PORSCHES
AT LE MANS

DOMINIQUE PASCAL

Foulis

Haynes

A FOULIS Motoring Book

This edition first published 1984

©E.P.A., Paris 1984

Published by:
Haynes Publishing Group
Sparkford, Yeovil, Somerset BA22 7JJ,
England

British Library Cataloging in
Publication Data

Pascal, Dominique
    Porsche at Le Mans.

    1. Porsche automobile – History
    I. Title
    629.2.'28   TL215.P75

    ISBN 0-85429-457-0

Porsche holds the undisputed record for the highest number of marque entries in the Le Mans 24 Hours. At the time of publication, 448 Porsches had competed in this prestigious event.

Through the pages of this book the reader will be able to follow the story of Porsches in the world's greatest endurance race from the début of the Porsche 356 to the amazing 956 Group C. The latter produces 650bhp compared with the 'mere' 46 bhp of the former – but this should not create a patronizing smile: the 356 required just as much courage and skill to drive as the 956 ...

I hope that all the Porsche drivers and mechanics will find an acknowledgement in this book, for they have played a very important role in the history of Le Mans.

D. Pascal

1951

One Porsche starts, one finishes

The first participation of Porsche at Le Mans occurred in 1951. Two 356s were entered, but the one that should have carried the number 47 was the victim of an accident in pre-race trials when driven by Rudolph Sauerwein. Bad weather conditions did not prevent the other little Porsche from finishing the race in 20th place, a long way behind the Jaguar C-Type of the British pair Walker and Whitehead who won the event, covering 3611.19km (2243.89 miles) at an average speed of 150.46km/h (93.49mph).

Porsche no. 46. A Type 356, entered by Porsche, and driven by A. Veuillet and E. Mouche. It was placed 20th on distance, having covered 2840.65km (1765.09 miles) at an average of 118.36km/h (73.54mph). It won its class (751 to 1100cc) and came fifth in the Index of Performance.

August Veuillet, the young importer of the new marque to France, drove a remarkably consistent race, helped by his friend Edmond Mouche, who had been his team mate in the 1949 event in a Delage. They lapped with almost clockwork regularity,

beating the coveted record for the shortest time in the pits. Refuelling was carried out without any serious problems and there was nothing to stop the progress of the Porsche, which beat the Bonnet-Bayol Mercedes-Benz in the same class.

This 356 was built at Porsche's first factory at Gmünd, in Austria. It developed 46bhp and could reach 160km/h (100mph). Its best lap was completed in 5m 44.7s, at 139.75km/h (86.83mph). Porsche had started on its conquest of Le Mans ...

Race no.	Type Model	Engine position	Number of cylinders	Capacity in cc	Bore & stroke in mm	Valve operation	Cooling	Induction	Brakes	Transmission	Body material	Weight in kg (lb)
46	356	Rear	Flat-4	1086	73.5 x 64	ohv	air	2 carb	Drums	Porsche 4+R	aluminium	640 (1411)

1952

Three Porsches start, one finishes

German industry was recovering well from the war. Less than ten years after the end of hostilities, Mercedes achieved a double at Le Mans with the famous 300SL. Lang and Riess, the winning team, covered a distance of 3733.80km (2320.07 miles) at an average of 155.57km/h (96.67mph). As for the Porsches, Veuillet and Mouche returned to try to win their class, and succeeded in doing so.

Porsche no. 51. Type 356, entered by Porsche KG, and driven by von Hanstein and Müller. It retired in the sixth hour, after being logged in 25th place in the previous hour. Gearbox trouble forced the retirement, leaving its Porsche stablemates to continue the race.

Porsche no. 50. Type 356, entered by Porsche KG, and driven by Veuillet and Mouche. It came 11th in the distance classification, covering 2955.41km (1836.407 miles) at an average of 123.14km/h (76.51mph). It was eighth in the Index of Performance.

Another achievement in the 1100cc class for the Veuillet-Mouche team, who bore Porsche's hopes after car no. 51 withdrew and no. 47 was put out of the race, was to beat the Dyna Panhard of Plantivaux and Chancel.

Porsche no. 47. Type 356, entered by Porsche KG, and driven by Lachaize and Martin. This car was disqualified in the 19th hour, after being in 14th place during the preceding hour.

The track stewards announced the disqualification of this car when the driver failed to switch the engine off during a refuelling stop. Until this time the Porsche had been lapping consistently and without mishap.

Race no.	Type Model	Engine position	Number of cylinders	Capacity in cc	Bore & stroke in mm	Valve operation	Cooling	Induction	Brakes	Transmission	Body material	Weight in kg (lb)
47	356	Rear	Flat-4			ohv	air	2 carb	Drums	Porsche 4+R	aluminium	–
50	356	Rear	Flat-4	1086	73.5 x 64	ohv	air	2 carb	Drums	Porsche 4+R	aluminium	–
51	356	Rear	Flat-4	1086	73.5 x 64	ohv	air	2 carb	Drums	Porsche 4+R	aluminium	–

1953

Four Porsches start, two finish

Although the four overhead camshaft engine was ready, the new Porsche 550s that lined up at the start had the older overhead-valve unit ... a wise decision However, one major innovation was registered on the eve of the 1953 Le Mans 24 Hours: the advent of the mid-engined Porsches, with their power units placed ahead of the rear axle and offset gearboxes.

Again it was a Jaguar C-Type, in the expert hands of Rolt and Hamilton, that won from another Jaguar C-type driven by Moss and Walker. The distance winners covered 4088.06km (2540.20 miles) at an average of 170.33km/h (105.842mph).

Porsche no. 45. Type 550 (chassis no. 550-02), entered by Porsche KG, and driven by von Frankenberg and P. Frère. It came 15th in the distance classification, covering 3332.03km (2070.427 miles) at an average 138.03km/h (85.76mph), and was 16th in the Index of Performance.

Throughout the race the two drivers (both journalists) had to grit their teeth and hold back as their car ran well and its mid-engined configuration gave a great advantage in road-holding. This Porsche was placed equal 16th with its stablemate no. 44 in the Index of Performance, but took 1st place in the 1500cc class.

Race no.	Type Model	Engine position	Number of cylinders	Capacity in cc	Bore & stroke in mm	Valve operation	Cooling	Induction	Brakes	Transmission	Body material	Weight in kg (lb)
44	550	Rear	Flat-4	1495	84.9 x 66	ohv	air	2 Solex	Drums	Porsche 4+R	aluminium	550 (1213)
45	550	Rear	Flat-4	1495	84.9 x 66	ohv	air	2 Solex	Drums	Porsche 4+R	aluminium	550 (1213)
46	356	Rear	Flat-4	1488	80 x 74	ohv	air	Solex	Drums	Porsche 4+R	–	–
49	356SL	Rear	Flat-4	1090	68.5 x 74	ohv	air	Solex	Drums	Porsche 4+R	–	–

Porsche no. 44. Type 550 (chassis no. 550-01), entered by Porsche KG, and driven by H. Herrmann and H. Glöckler. It was placed 16th equal in the distance classification, covering 3330.64km (2069.56 miles) at an average of 138.77km/h (86.23mph). It also came 16th in the Index of Performance.

Hans Herrmann, a Stuttgart confectioner and Glöckler's partner was, like the other Porsche drivers, under the command of a new racing manager, the well-known Huschke von Hanstein: he paced the two 550s, which crossed the finishing line together.

Porsche no. 46. Type 356, entered by Gonzague Olivier, and driven by Olivier and Martin. It withdrew in the 18th hour, after being logged in 33rd place in the preceding hour. The only privately-owned Porsche in the 1953 event, this car had engine failure after moving through the field 39th to 25th place in the overall classification.

Porsche no. 49. Type 356SL, entered by Porsche KG, and driven by Veuillet and Müller. It retired in the 18th hour, after being logged in 31st place during the preceding hour. This works-entered Porsche was let down by its engine.

An old model, this 356SL had set out to ensure success for Porsche in the 1500cc class, but fate decreed otherwise ....

1954

Four Porsches start, two finish

The Porsche 1500cc dohc engines were now ready to allow Porsche to tackle their rivals in this category, the Italian OSCAs. There was a duel at the front of the field between Jaguars and Ferraris: one of the latter won the event. The winner, a Ferrari 375 'Plus', was driven by the Frenchman Maurice Trintignant and the Argentine Froilan Gonzalez, and covered 4061.15km (2523.48 miles) in 24 hours, at an average speed of 169.21km/h (105.14mph). This was not quite as good as the previous year (it rained a lot in 1954), when the 4000km (2485 mile) threshold had been passed for the first time, by the Rolt-Hamilton Jaguar.

Porsche no. 39. Type 550 (chassis no. 550-12), entered by Porsche KG, and driven by J. Claes and Stasse. It was placed 12th on distance, covering 3064.13km (1903.96 miles) at an average of 127.67km/h (79.33mph). It came 17th in the Index of Performance.

This Porsche profited from the OSCAs' fratricidal struggle. Less than two hours from the end the two OSCAs, which had already secured the marque's victory in their class and, believing themselves safe, were fighting it out between themselves, had an accident. One of them was able to restart, but was eliminated by a steward. This dramatic turn of events, so common at Le Mans, left the field clear for the Porsche to win the 1500cc class.

Porsche no. 47. Type 550 (chassis no. 550-13), entered by Porsche KG, and driven by G. Olivier and Duntov. It was placed 14th for distance, covering 2902.26km (1803.38 miles) in 24 hours, at an average 120.92km/h (75.14mph). It was also 14th in the Index of Performance. The only 1100cc Porsche entered, it won its class after a very intelligent race without incident, except for some minor gearbox troubles.

Race no.	Type Model	Engine position	Number of cylinders	Capacity in cc	Bore & stroke in mm	Valve operation	Cooling	Induction	Brakes	Transmission	Body material	Weight in kg (lb)
39	550	Rear	Flat-4	1498	85 x 66	4 ohc	air	2 Weber	Drums	Porsche 4+R	aluminium	680 (1500) wet
40	550	Rear	Flat-4	1498	85 x 66	4 ohc	air	2 Weber	Drums	Porsche 4+R	aluminium	680 (1500) wet
41	550	Rear	Flat-4	1498	85 x 66	4 ohc	air	2 Weber	Drums	Porsche 4+R	aluminium	680 (1500) wet
47	550	Rear	Flat-4	1089.3	72.5 x 66	–	air	2 Weber	Drums	Porsche 4+R	aluminium	680 (1500) wet

Porsche no. 41. Type 550 (chassis no. 550-11), entered by Porsche KG, and driven by H. Herrmann and Polensky. It retired in the 14th hour, after being logged in 7th place in the preceding hour. Fitted like no. 40 with the new dohc engine, this Porsche suffered the same fate as its companion. Defective ignition caused the retirement of both cars.

Porsche no. 40. Type 550 (chassis no. 550-10), entered by Porsche KG, and driven by von Frankenberg and Glöckler. It was withdrawn in the first hour of the race. Afflicted with the same trouble as no. 41, this car did not go far, not even passing the one-hour mark. However, it had been the fastest of the Porsches, exceeding 211km/h (131mph) on the Hunaudières straight.

1955

Six Porsches start, five finish

This was the year of the appalling accident that had so profound an effect on the public opinion about motor racing and, of course, this tragedy cast a shadow over Porsche's first victory in the Index of Performance. Hawthorn and Bueb were the outright winners in a Jaguar D-Type which, at the end of the 24 hours, had covered 4135.38km (2569.60 miles) at an average of 172.30 km/h (107.06mph).

Porsche no. 37. Type 550 (chassis no. 550-0046), entered by Porsche KG, and driven by Polensky and von Frankenberg. It came fourth in the distance classification, covering 3829.73km (2379.68 miles) in 24 hours, at an average of 159.57km/h (99.15mph). This car also came first in the Index of Performance.

Unfortunately, victory in the Index and in the 1500cc class were overshadowed by the tragic events that had taken place on the straight in front of the pits, so these wins passed relatively unnoticed by those present.

Porsche no. 66. Type 550 (chassis no. 550-0015), entered by the Ecurie Belge, and driven by Seidel Sind Gendebien. It came fifth in distance, covering 3715.55km (2308.73 miles) in 24 hours at an average of 154.81km/h (96.19mph). It was fourth in the Index of Performance.

This was Olivier Gendebien's first participation in the Le Mans 24 Hours, and he obtained a superb performance by this car, which was placed among the nicely grouped Porsches that finished fourth, fifth and sixth in the 1955 event.

Porsche no. 62. Type 550 (chassis no. 550-0047), entered by Porsche KG, and driven by H. Glöckler and Juhan. It was placed sixth in distance, covering 3679.67km (2286.44 miles) in 24 hours at an average of 153.32km/h (95.26mph). It came fifth in the Index of Performance and third in the 1500cc class, behind the two other Porsches of the same capacity.

Porsche no. 65. Type 550 (chassis no. 550-0016), entered by G. Olivier, and driven by Olivier and Jeser. It was placed 18th in distance, covering 3155.31km (1960.61 miles) in 24 hours at an average of 131.47km/h (81.69mph). It was sixteenth in the Index of Performance. This car was the last of the Porsches to finish. It was a private entry, helped considerably by the factory.

Porsche no. 49. Type 550 (chassis no. 550-0048), entered by Porsche KG, and driven by A. Duntov and Veuillet. It was placed 13th in distance, covering 3303.57km (2052.74 miles) in 24 hours at an average of 137.64km/h (85.53mph). It was tenth in the Index of Performance.

In addition to the victories in the Index of Performance and the 1500cc class, the Porsche team also won the 1100cc class, thanks to this car, which was driven with consistency and intelligence: the only car in its class to finish. Its rivals Arnott, Panhard, Cooper and Lotus all had to retire. This was to be Veuillet's last appearance at Le Mans as a driver.

Porsche no. 38. Type 550 (chassis no. 550-003), entered by W. Riggenberg, and driven by Riggenberg and Gilomen. It retired in the eighth hour, after being in 39th position in the preceding hour. This car, with its Swiss drivers, was the only Porsche out of six entries not to reach the finish in 1955: piston trouble was responsible for the retirement.

Race no.	Type Model	Engine position	Number of cylinders	Capacity in cc	Bore & stroke in mm	Valve operation	Cooling	Induction	Brakes	Transmission	Body material	Weight in kg (lb)
37	550	Rear	Flat-4	1498	85 x 66	4 ohc	air	2 Solex	Drums	Porsche 4+R	aluminium	–
38	550	Rear	Flat-4	1498	86 x 66	4 ohc	air	2 Solex	Drums	Porsche 4+R	aluminium	–
49	550	Rear	Flat-4	1089	72.5 x 66	–	air	2 Solex	Drums	Porsche 4+R	aluminium	–
62	550	Rear	Flat-4	1498	85 x 66	4 ohc	air	2 Solex	Drums	Porsche 4+R	aluminium	–
65	550	Rear	Flat-4	1089	72.5 x 66	–	air	2 Solex	Drums	Porsche 4+R	aluminium	–
66	550	Rear	Flat-4	1498	86 x 66	4 ohc	air	2 Solex	Drums	Porsche 4+R	aluminium	–

1956

Six Porsches start, two finish

Following the catastrophe of the preceding year, a vast amount of work was done on the circuit to make it safer. In addition, the regulations were altered with the aim of reducing the speed of the competitors and also their fuel consumption. The only record broken was in the number of withdrawals —14 cars finished out of 49 starters — and perhaps, too, the awful weather. The circuit soon turned into a skating rink and a succession of cars left the track. In these atrocious conditions only a third of the cars from the Porsche camp reached the finishing line.

The winners, in a Jaguar D-Type, were the Scots Sanderson and Flockhart who covered 4034.92km (2507.18 miles) at an average of 168.12km/h (104.46mph).

Porsche no. 25. Type 550 A (chassis no. 550A-0104), entered by Porsche KG, and driven by von Frankenberg and von Trips. It was placed fifth on distance, covering 3792.24km (2356.394 miles) in 24 hours at an average of 158.01km/h (98.18mph), and second in the Index of Performance.

This Porsche had an interesting race, bracketed by Mercedes, but eventually breaking away to get the Index of Performance. It should be noted that of the two drivers von Trips proved to be particularly fast, lapping at more than 173km/h (107mph).

Porsche no. 34. Type 356 A (chassis no. 56007), entered by Bourel, and driven by Bourel and Slotine. It was placed 13th on distance covering 2852.64km (1771.93 miles) in 24 hours at an average of 118.81 km/h (73.83mph). This Carrera achieved the dubious distinction of finishing last but one, in front of a V.P. Renault. The Frenchmen were not placed in the Index of Performance but, given the few survivors in this year's Le Mans 24 Hours, finishing was an achievement!

Porsche no. 24. Type 550 A (chassis number 550A-0103), entered by Porsche KG, and driven by Maglioli and Herrmann. It retired in the 16th hour, after being in 17th place in the preceding hour. This second works 550 A was not as fast as no. 25: its drivers seemed to have less sparkle. The car's retirement was because of piston trouble, leaving the von Trips-von Frankenberg Porsche to take the Index of Performance from Mercedes.

Porsche no. 28. Type 550 (chassis no. 550-0032), entered by G. Olivier, and driven by Storez and Polensky. It withdrew in the eighth hour, after being in 36th place during the preceding hour. This French-entered and French-driven blue Porsche left the race with distributor trouble.

Porsche no. 26. Type Carrera 1500, entered by Porsche KG, and driven by Nathan and Glöckler. It retired in the ninth hour, after being logged in 29th place in the preceding hour.

It was at 9.45pm that Glöckler, who was then driving, saw Meyrat's Ferrari ahead of him, but facing the wrong way! A collision was unavoidable. The Porsche overturned and caught fire on the straight between Maison Blanche and the pits. Glöckler was pulled from the flames with a broken leg.

Porsche no. 27. Type 550 (chassis no. 550-041), entered by W. Seidel, and driven by Hezemans and de Beaufort. It withdrew in the seventh hour, after being logged in 36th place in the preceding hour. The Dutchmen's car was the first of the Porsches to leave the race, suffering from suspension problems.

Race no.	Type Model	Engine position	Number of cylinders	Capacity in cc	Bore & stroke in mm	Valve operation	Cooling	Induction	Brakes	Transmission	Body material	Weight in kg (lb)
24	550A	Rear	Flat-4	1498	85 x 66	4 ohc	air	2 Weber	Drums	Porsche 5+R	aluminium	–
25	550A	Rear	Flat-4	1498	85 x 66	4 ohc	air	2 Weber	Drums	Porsche 5+R	aluminium	–
26	Carrera 1500	Rear	Flat-4	1498	85 x 66	4 ohc	air	2 Weber	Drums	Porsche 4+R	aluminium	–
27	550	Rear	Flat-4	1498	85 x 66	4 ohc	air	2 Weber	Drum	Porsche 4+R	aluminium	–
28	550	Rear	Flat-4	1498	85 x 66	4 ohc	air	2 Weber	Drums	Porsche 4+R	aluminium	–
34	356A	Rear	Flat-4	1290	74.5 x 74	–	air	2 Solex	Drums	Porsche 4+R	aluminium	–

1957

Six Porsches start, one finishes

All the records were broken in the 1957 Le Mans 24 Hours: distance, lap and class records!

Of the six Porsches that started one finished — and once again it was a privately-entered car. The overall winners in 1957 were Flockhart and Bueb in a Jaguar D-Type, covering 4397.10km (2732.23 miles) at an average of 183.21km/h (113.84mph).

Porsche no. 35. Type 550 A (chassis no. 550A-0132), entered by E. Hugus, and driven by Hugus and de Beaufort. It was placed eighth on distance, covering 3848.35km (2391.25 miles) in 24 hours at an average of 160.34km/h (99.63mph).

This Porsche in American colours — white with blue bands — was the only one to reach the finish: a private entry that saved the Porsche line-up from total rout. Victory for this car in the 1500cc class, preserved some lustre for the marque in an otherwise disappointing race. Even so, the Lotus 1100, which finished behind the Porsche and also won its class, could have been very dangerous ...

Porsche no. 34. Type 550A (chassis no. 550A-0120), entered by Porsche KG, and driven by Storez and Crawford. It retired in the 23rd hour, after being logged in seventh place in the preceding hour. The last Porsche to leave the race, less than one hour from the finish, it ran out of fuel! The Frenchman Storez, who was then at the wheel, pushed his car to the pits — but in vain. The engine was dead and could not be restarted, which left the solitary Hugus-de Beaufort Porsche to finish the race.

15

Porsche no. 32. Type 718 RS (chassis no. 718-001), entered by Porsche KG, and driven by Maglioli and E. Barth. It retired in the 12th hour, after being in 11th place in the preceding hour.

A great deal was expected of this new light-weight model with its tubular chassis, and new front end. Another detail was the oil-cooler integral with the front bonnet; and the brakes were larger in diameter than those on the 550s. This new car proved very fast in Maglioli's hands, lapping once at 181.63km/h (112.86mph): close to the average speed of the winning Jaguar. The car was well placed when, leaving the Tertre Rouge, it collided with Tony Brooks' Aston Martin.

Porsche no. 60. Type 356 A (chassis no. 550-0082), entered by the Belgian national team, and driven by Dubois and Hacquin. It was disqualified in the eighth hour, after being in 37th place in the preceding hour.

Porsche no. 33. Type 550A (chassis no. 550A-0131), entered by Porsche KG, and driven by Herrmann and von Frankenberg. It retired in the eighth hour after being in the 13th place during the preceding hour. The second Porsche to leave the race, this 550 A had ignition troubles that gradually worsened.

Porsche no. 36. Type 356 A (chassis no. 83203), entered by Slotine, and driven by Slotine and Bourel. It withdrew in the fourth hour, after being in 48th place in the preceding hour. The first Porsche to retire, this French-entered 356 suffered from piston trouble.

Race no.	Type Model	Engine position	Number of cylinders	Capacity in cc	Bore & stroke in mm	Valve operation	Cooling	Induction	Brakes	Transmission	Body material	Weight in kg (lb)
32	718RS	Rear	Flat-4	1498	85 x 66	4 ohc	air	2 Weber	Drums	Porsche 5+R	aluminium	570 (1257)
33	550A	Rear	Flat-4	1498	85 x 66	4 ohc	air	2 Weber	Drums	Porsche 5+R	aluminium	—
34	550A	Rear	Flat-4	1498	85 x 66	4 ohc	air	2 Weber	Drums	Porsche 5+R	aluminium	—
35	550A	Rear	Flat-4	1498	85 x 66	4 ohc	air	2 Weber	Drums	Porsche 5+R	aluminium	—
36	356A	Rear	Flat-4	1498	85 x 66	—	air	2 Weber	Drums	Porsche 4+R	—	—
60	356A	Rear	Flat-4	1498	85 x 66	—	air	2 Weber	Drums	Porsche 5+R	—	—

1958

Five Porsches start, four finish

A lucky year for Porsche: with the help of talented drivers it thrashed the pre-race favourites. Who would have thought that the Porsche RSKs could worry the Aston Martins? Four out of five Porches finished and were well placed behind the overall winners, Oliver Gendebien and Phil Hill, who covered 4101.92 (2548.81 miles) in their Ferrari 250 Testa Rossa at an average of 170.91km/h (106.20mph), despite the torrential rain that fell on the circuit during the night.

Porsche no. 29. Type 718 RSK (chassis no. 718.005), entered by Porsche KG, and driven by Behra and Herrmann. It was placed third on distance, covering 3909.64km (2429.34 miles) in 24 hours at an average of 162.90km/h (101.22mph), and seventh in the Index of Performance.

A superb race by Behra and Herrmann who from the fourth hour of the event were lying sixth, amongst the big-capacity cars. The French champion showed tremendous spirit. He lapped in 4m 20.5s — very fast when it is realized that Moss, in a 3-litre Aston Martin, conceded less than 10s. Second place overall eluded this crack team because of brake problems, but in addition to third place in the general classification, Porsche no. 29 won the 2-litre class.

Porsche no. 31. Type 718 RSK (chassis no. 718-003), entered by Porsche KG, and driven by E. Barth and P. Frère. It was placed fourth in distance, covering 3895.18km (2420.35 miles) in 24 hours at an average of 162.34km/h (100.87mph), and was fifth in the Index of Performance. This team drove a very intelligent race, adhering strictly to the race plans and staying behind Behra and Herrmann, the team leaders. It won the 1500cc class.

Porsche no. 34. Type 550 A (chassis no. 550A-0142), entered by Colas, and driven by Kerguen and Dewez. It was placed sixth in distance, covering 3415.16km (2122.08 miles) in 24 hours at an average of 142.29km/h (88.42mph), and 13th in the Index of Performance.
This privately-entered Spyder, with its French drivers, was in danger of losing the reward for its persistence when it ran off the road at Mulsanne and became stuck. Fortunately it eventually succeeded in freeing itself and rejoining the race.

Porsche no. 32. Type 550 A (chassis no. 550A-0145), entered by Carel Godin de Beaufort, and driven by Beaufort and Linge. It was fifth in the distance classification, covering 3869.26km (2402.24 miles) in 24 hours at an average of 161.21 km/h (100.17mph), and came sixth in the Index of Performance. Like those of no. 31, this car's drivers shrewdly followed the Porsche race plan, achieving a high level of consistency and finishing second in class.

Porsche no. 30. Type 718 RSK (chassis no. 718-004), entered by Porsche KG, and driven by von Frankenberg and Storez. It retired in the ninth hour, after being in 32nd place during the preceding hour. The only Porsche to retire, no. 30, with its Franco-German team, crashed into the barriers at Tertre Rouge in frightful weather conditions: von Frankenberg was at the wheel.

Race no.	Type Model	Engine position	Number of cylinders	Capacity in cc	Bore & stroke in mm	Valve operation	Cooling	Induction	Brakes	Transmission	Body material	Weight in kg (lb)
29	718RSK	Rear	Flat-4	1587.5	87.5 x 66	4 ohc	air	2 Weber	Drums	Porsche 5+R	aluminium	–
30	718RSK	Rear	Flat-4	1587.5	87.5 x 66	4 ohc	air	2 Weber	Drums	Porsche 5+R	aluminium	–
31	718RSK	Rear	Flat-4	1498	85 x 66	4 ohc	air	2 Weber	Drums	Porsche 5+R	aluminium	–
32	550A	Rear	Flat-4	1498	85 x 66	4 ohc	air	2 Weber	Drums	Porsche 4+R	aluminium	–
34	550A	Rear	Flat-4	1498	85 x 66	4 ohc	air	2 Weber	Drums	Porsche 5+R	aluminium	–

1959

Six Porsches start, none finish

This was Aston Martin's year at Le Mans. Although Moss started out at the front, it was the shrewder Shelby-Salvadori team who were first across the line, having covered a distance of 4347.90km (2701.66 miles) at an average of 181.16km/h (112.56mph). For Porsche, accustomed since its first participation in the event to class victories, this year was fruitless. In fact none of the six Porsches that started completed the race. Technically the cars had developed year by year, but the 1959 Porsches all suffered mechanical faults and retired one after the other. Winning no points at Le Mans, Porsche had no further hope of the World Championship in this year.

Porsche no. 35. Type 550 RS (chassis no. 550A-0142), entered by Kerguen, and driven by Kerguen and Lacaze. It retired in the 20th hour, after being logged in ninth place in the preceding hour. For a while this was the only Porsche left in the race, but not for long — this sole 550 entry gave up just a few minutes after the Americans in no. 37 had stopped. There was nothing left to do but get out the toolboxes!

Porsche no. 37. Type 718 RSK (chassis no. 718-024), entered by Hugus, and driven by Hugus and Ericksson. It retired in the 20th hour, after being in fourth place in the preceding hour. After the leading Porsches had retired, this American team's car accelerated and for a while threatened the Mercedes that was leading the Index of Performance. A valve fault decided things otherwise and allowed the Mercedes to take the coveted Index.

Race no.	Type Model	Engine position	Number of cylinders	Capacity in cc	Bore & stroke in mm	Valve operation	Cooling	Induction	Brakes	Transmission	Body material	Weight in kg (lb)
31	718RSK	Rear	Flat-4	1587.5	87.5 x 66	4 ohc	air	2 Weber	Drums	Porsche 5+R	aluminium	540 (1257)
32	718RSK	Rear	Flat-4	1587.5	87.5 x 66	4 ohc	air	2 Weber	Drums	Porsche 5+R	aluminium	–
34	718RSK	Rear	Flat-4	1498	85 x 66	4 ohc	air	2 Weber	Drums	Porsche 5+R	aluminium	–
35	550RS	Rear	Flat-4	1498	85 x 66	4 ohc	air	2 Weber	Drums	Porsche 5+R	aluminium	–
36	718RSK	Rear	Flat-4	1498	85 x 66	4 ohc	air	2 Weber	Drums	Porsche 5+R	aluminium	540 (1257)
37	718RSK	Rear	Flat-4	1498	85 x 66	4 ohc	air	2 Weber	Drums	Porsche 5+R	aluminium	576 (1270)

Porsche no. 36. Type 718 RSK (chassis no. 718-027), entered by Carel Godin de Beaufort, and driven by Beaufort and Heinz. It retired in the 15th hour, after being logged in fourth place in the preceding hour. The Dutchman de Beaufort chose a Brazilian team mate for this year's Le Mans, but a crankshaft breakage destroyed their ambitions.

Porsche no. 34. Type 718 RSK (chassis no. 718-006), entered by Porsche KG, and driven by E. Barth and Seidel. It withdrew in the fourteenth hour, after being in sixth place in the preceding hour. No. 34 was the last of the works Porsches left in the race after nos. 32 and 31 had retired. However, it too succumbed to mechanical problems a few minutes later; this time gearbox trouble.

Porsche no. 31. Type 718 RSK (chassis no. 718-008), entered by Porsche KG, and driven by Bonnier and von Trips. It retired in the 14th hour, after being in fourth place in the preceding hour. Bonnier was the fastest of the Porsche drivers, achieving 188.41km/h (117.07mph), but he too had to give up. After no. 32 had retired, this Porsche took the lead in the Index, but not for long. It had to withdraw with clutch trouble. A pity for it had been well placed at the time.

Porsche no. 32. Type 718 RSK (chassis no. 718-007), entered by Porsche KG, and driven by Herrmann and Maglioli. It retired in the sixth hour, after being in ninth place in the preceding hour. The first Porsche to retire, with valve trouble, the Herrmann-Maglioli car was for a time (in the third hour) in the lead of the Index of Performance.

1960

Six Porsches start, two finish

This year marked the beginning of the Ferrari era in the Le Mans 24 hours. The Frère-Gendebien Testa Rossa won the event at an average speed of 175.73km/h (109.19mph), covering 4217.52km (2620.65 miles). This year also saw the appearance in GT racing of the Carrera Abarths developing 135bhp and the RS60s, a development of the 718 RSK, lighter but with a lengthened wheelbase. For Porsche it was a slightly better year than 1959, with a minor Le Mans class vistory to its credit.

Porsche no. 35. Type 1600 GS (chassis no. 1001), entered by Porsche KG, and driven by Linge and H. Walter. It was placed sixth in the distance classification, covering 3619.75km (2249.21 miles) in 24 hours at an average of 150.82km/h (93.71mph) and 13th in the Index of Performance.

This car was Porsche's salvation. Rebodied and lightened by Abarth and Reuter on a 356B base, it was homologated for GT racing when 25 examples were manufactured. It won its class, overtaking the no. 39 Porsche, which was suffering from gearbox problems.

Porsche no. 39. Type RS60 (chassis no. 718-042), entered by Porsche KG, and driven by Barth and Seidel. It came 11th in the distance classification, covering 3552.45km (2207.39 miles) in 24 hours at an average of 148.01km/h (91.97mph). It also took 20th place in the Index of Performance and 9th in the Index of Efficiency.

This car very nearly did not finish. Problems with the gearbox deprived its drivers of three out of five gears! Despite these troubles it managed to get to the finish, but was passed by Carrera Abarth.

Porsche no. 33. Type RS60 (chassis no. 718-044), entered by Porsche KG, and driven by Bonnier and Hill. It retired in the 18th hour, having been in 14th place in the preceding hour. This was the fastest of the Porsches before it pulled out with a cracked piston.

Porsche no. 36. Type RS60, entered by Kerguen and driven by Kerguen and Lacaze. It retired in the eighth hour, after being in 16th place in the preceding hour. Distributor trouble caused this French team to withdraw.

Porsche no. 38. Type RS60 (chassis no. 718-055), entered by Beaufort and driven by Beaufort and Stoop. It retired in the 17th hour, after being in 16th place in the preceding hour. A defective distributor put it out of the race.

Porsche no. 34. Type RS60 (chassis no. 718-043), entered by Porsche KG and driven by Trintignant and Herrmann. It retired in the sixth hour, after being in 18th place in the preceding hour. A broken connecting rod caused this team to abandon the race.

Race no.	Type Model	Engine position	Number of cylinders	Capacity in cc	Bore & stroke in mm	Valve operation	Cooling	Induction	Brakes	Transmission	Body material	Weight in kg (lb)
33	RS60	Rear	Flat-4	1605.6	88 x 66	4 ohc	air	2 Weber	Drums	Porsche 5+R	aluminium	–
34	RS60	Rear	Flat-4	1605.6	88 x 66	4 ohc	air	2 Weber	Drums	Porsche 5+R	aluminium	–
35	1600GS	Rear	Flat-4	1588	87.5 x 66	4 ohc	air	2 Solex	Drums	Porsche 4+R	aluminium	778 (1716)
36	RS60	Rear	Flat-4	1588	87.5 x 66	4 ohc	air	2 Weber	Drums	Porsche 5+R	aluminium	–
38	RS60	Rear	Flat-4	1588	87.5 x 66	4 ohc	air	2 Weber	Drums	Porsche 5+R	aluminium	582 (1283)
39	RS60	Rear	Flat-4	1498	85 x 66	4 ohc	air	2 Weber	Drums	Porsche	aluminium	–

1961

Five Porsches start, three finish

No one could rival the Ferraris this year and Olivier Gendebien repeated his victory, teamed as in 1958 with the American Phil Hill, who was Formula One World champion in 1961. The Belgo-American pair broke the distance record, covering 4476.58km (2781.60 miles) at an average of 186.52km/h (115.90mph). Porsche entered five cars, one of them a new coupé based on the 718 and designed by one of Ferdinand Porsche's sons.

Porsche no. 33. Type RS61 (chassis no. 718-047), entered by Porsche System and driven by Gregory and Holbert. It was placed fifth in distance, covering 4154.46km (2581.46 miles) in 24 hours at an average of 163.10km/h (107.56mph), and sixth in the Index of Performance.

The best of the Porsches, and first in the 2-litre class, it slotted itself into fifth place among the Italians (Ferrari first, third and sixth, Maserati fourth).

Porsche no. 32. Type RS61 (chassis no. 718-045), entered by Porsche System and driven by E. Barth and Herrmann. It came seventh in the distance classification, covering 4112.29km (2555.25 miles) in 24 hours at an average of 171.34km/h (106.46mph), and was third in the Index of Performance.

This Porsche was fourth in the Index of Efficiency after an uneventful race.

Porsche no. 36. Type 695 GS (chassis no. 1013) GT class, entered by Porsche System and driven by Linge and Ben Pon. It was placed 10th in the distance classification, covering 3818.67km (2372.81 miles) in 24 hours at an average of 159.11km/h (98.86mph), and 11th in the Index of Performance. The only Porsche GT to finish, it won the 1600cc class and secured fifth place in the Index of Efficiency.

Porsche no. 37. Type 695 (chassis no. 1002) GT class, entered by Veuillet, driven by Buchet and P. Monneret. It retired in the 23rd hour, after being in 12th place in the preceding hour.

Porsches entered, but fate decided otherwise. No. 32 retired an hour before the end of the event, followed by the Frenchmen in their blue car no. 37, put out by engine failure.

It should have been possible to witness a group finish by the five

Porsche no. 30. Type RS61 (chassis no. 718-046), entered by Porsche System and driven by Bonnier and Gurney. It retired in the 23rd hour, after being in 11th place in the preceding hour. Gurney, who was then at the wheel, had to withdraw very close

to the end with a broken crankshaft, after a very intelligently conducted and consistent race.

Race no.	Type Model	Engine position	Number of cylinders	Capacity in cc	Bore & stroke in mm	Valve operation	Cooling	Induction	Brakes	Transmission	Body material	Weight in kg (lb)
30	RS61-718	Rear	Flat-4	1679	90 x 66	4 ohc	air	2 Weber	Drums	Porsche 5+R	aluminium	630 (1389)
32	RS61-718	Rear	Flat-4	1606	88 x 66	4 ohc	air	2 Weber	Drums	Porsche 5+R	aluminium	630 (1389)
33	RS61-718	Rear	Flat-4	1967	92 x 74	4 ohc	air	2 Weber	Drums	Porsche 5+R	aluminium	630 (1389)
36	695GS	Rear	Flat-4	1588	87.5 x 66	4 ohc	air	2 Solex	Drums	Porsche 4+R	aluminium	–
37	695GS	Rear	Flat-4	1588	87.5 x 66	4 ohc	air	2 Weber	Drums	Porsche 4+R	aluminium	–

1962

Three Porsches start, two finish

There was a change in the rules for the Le Mans 24 Hours in this year. The World Championship was now open to GT cars and experimental cars of up to 4-litres capacity could now compete at Le Mans. It was one of these cars that won: the Ferrari 330LM of Phil Hill and Olivier Gendebien, which covered 4451.25km (2765.88 miles) in 24 hours, at an average of 185.46km/h (115.24mph).

Porsche was playing seriously in the world championship stakes and three Porsche GTs were present at the start.

Porsche no. 34. Type 695 GS Abarth, GT class, entered by Porsche System and driven by Barth and Herrmann. It came seventh in distance, covering 3858.53km (2397.58 miles) in 24 hours at an average of 160.77km/h (99.90mph), and ninth in the Index of Performance and fifth in the Index of Efficiency.

This car carried off the victory in its class despite gearbox trouble and the assault of the little Lotus Elite 1300, which often worried and, at one stage, even overtook the Porsche.

Porsche no. 35. Type 695 GS Abarth (chassis no. 1013), GT class, entered by Veuillet and driven by Buchet and Schiller. It was placed 12th in the distance classification, covering 3655.69km (2271.54 miles) in 24 hours at an average of 152.32km/h (94.64mph), and fourth in the Index of Performance.

This traditional Porsche, entered by the French importer of the marque, drove from 28th to 12th place in the overall classification — but it was still a long way from Behra's Sports Porsche amongst the leaders.

Porsche no. 30. Type 695 GS Abarth (chassis no. 1010), GT class, entered by Porsche System and driven by de Beaufort and Ben Pon. It retired in the fourth hour, after being in 29th place in the preceding hour. This was the only Porsche to retire, after fuel feed and then transmission troubles.

Race no.	Type Model	Engine position	Number of cylinders	Capacity in cc	Bore & stroke in mm	Valve operation	Cooling	Induction	Brakes	Transmission	Body material	Weight in kg (lb)
30	695GS	Rear	Flat-4	1588	87.5 x 66	2 ohc	air	2 Solex	Drums	Porsche 4+R	aluminium	–
34	695GS	Rear	Flat-4	1588	87.5 x 66	4 ohc	air	2 Solex	Drums	Porsche 4+R	aluminium	–
35	695GS	Rear	Flat-4	1588	87.5 x 66	2 ohc	air	2 Solex	Drums	Porsche 4+R	aluminium	–

1963

Four Porsches start, one finishes

The most remarkable of the competing cars this year was undoubtedly the Rover turbine, which completed the course. At the end of the race there were six Ferraris in the first six places. The best of these was the 250P of Scarfiotti and Bandini — 4561.71km (2834.51 miles) at an average of 190.07km/h (118.10mph). Two 8-cylinder Porsches and two Carrera GT 200 GSs were entered, and there was one class victory for the marque. Note that it was thanks to Formula One that the Porsche 8-cylinder engine saw the light of day.

Porsche no. 28. Type 718/8 (chassis no. 718-047), entered by Porsche System and driven by Barth and Linge. It came eighth in distance, covering 4050.25km (2516.70 miles) in 24 hours at an average of 168.76km/h (121.56mph), and fifth in the Index of Performance and tenth in the Index of Efficiency.

The only finisher of the four Porsches, no. 28, had a brush with disaster when it lost a rear wheel. Fortunately Barth managed to push the car to the pits, but lost a great deal of time. Nevertheless, the car won the 2-litre class. Without the incident with the wheel no. 28 could well have finished two places better.

Porsche no. 27. Type 718/8 (chassis no. 718-046), entered by Porsche System and driven by Bonnier and Maggs. It was put out of the event in the ninth hour, after being in seventh place in the preceding hour. Bonnier was at the wheel when no. 27 had to retire. Ahead of him the engine of Penske's Ferrari had blown up. Blinded by smoke, Bonnier left the track, damaging the car to such an extent that it was immobilized and written off.

Porsche no. 30. Type 200 GS (chassis no. 122-992), entered by Porsche System and driven by Ben Pon and Schiller. It retired in the 10th hour, shortly after Koch's Carerra gave up, after being in 15th place in the preceding hour. The cause of retirement was an engine fault.

Porsche no. 29. Type 2000 GS, GT class (chassis no. 122-991), entered by Porsche System and driven by Koch and de Beaufort. It retired in the eighth hour, after being logged in 18th place in the preceding hour.

The two GT Porsches were the first to go, and both for the same reason: engine failure.

Race no.	Type Model	Engine position	Number of cylinders	Capacity in cc	Bore & stroke in mm	Valve operation	Cooling	Induction	Brakes	Transmission	Body material	Weight in kg (lb)
27	718/8	Rear	Flat-8	1981.5	76 x 54	2 ohc	air	4 Weber	–	6+R	aluminium	–
28	718/8	Rear	Flat-8	1981.5	76 x 54	2 ohc	air	4 Weber	–	6+R	aluminium	–
29	2000GS	Rear	Flat-4	1967.7	92 x 74	2 ohc	air	2 Weber	–	4+R	aluminium	825 (1819)
30	2000GS	Rear	Flat-4	1967.7	92 x 74	2 ohc	air	2 Weber	–	4+R	aluminium	825 (1819)

1964

Seven Porsches start, five finish

This was the 31st Le Mans 24 Hours. There was a record 350,000 spectators around the course, drawn by the first leg of the Ford-Ferrari duel, which was to go in favour of the Italians.

It was Ferrari's eighth Le Mans victory and its fifth consecutive win. Jean Guichet and Nono Vaccarrella at the wheel of their Ferrari prototype covered 4695.31km (2917.53 miles) in the course of the 24 hours, at an average 195.63km/h (121.56mph).

The novelty from Porsche was the new 904, introduced in December 1963, with 8-cylinder (prototype) or 4-cylinder (GT) engines. The other feature of this year's race was the record number of Porsches entered — eight — in the event.

Porsche no. 34. Type 904 GTS, GT class, entered by Veuillet and driven by Buchet and Ligier. It came seventh in the distance classification, covering 4344.59km (2699.60 miles) in 24 hours at an average of 181.02km/h (112.48mph). It was also third in the Index of Performance and equal seventh in the Index of Efficiency.

After the two 8-cylinder cars had retired this was the best-placed Porsche, beating the other 4-cylinder cars.

Porsche no. 31. Type 904 GTS, GT class, entered by Porsche System and driven by Schiller and Koch. It came tenth in the distance classification, covering 4227.52km (2626.85 miles) in 24 hours at an average of 176.14km/h (109.45mph). It achieved 12th place in the Index of Performance and 9th in the Index of Efficiency.

This, the third of the official Porsche entries, drove an intelligent race and was the only one to finish.

Porsche no. 33. Type 904 GTS, GT class, entered by Racing Team Holland and driven by Ben Pon and van Zalinge. It was placed eighth in distance, covering 4281.31km (2660.28 miles) in 24 hours at an average of 178.38km/h (110.84mph). It was also sixth in the Index of Performance and fifth in the Index of Efficiency.

This Porsche followed no. 34 like a shadow for the whole of the race. It was timed at 258km/h (160mph) on the Hunaudières straight during the race and in practice it achieved the best time of the five 904 GTS 4-cylinder Porsches.

Porsche no. 35. Type 904 GTS, GT class, entered by Scuderia Filipinetti and driven by Müller and C. Sage. It was placed 11th in distance, covering 4155.83km (2582.31 miles) in 24 hours at an average of 173.16km/h (107.59mph). It was also 14th in the Index of Performance and 4th in the Index of Efficiency. It had been a long time since a car entered by a Swiss team had been placed in the Le Mans 24 Hours.

Porsche no. 32. Type 904 GTS, Prototype class, entered by 'Franc' and driven by 'Franc' and Kerguen. It was placed 12th in distance, covering 4142.77km in 24 hours (2574.19 miles) at an average of 172.61km/h (107.25mph), and 15th in the Index of Performance. This was the second of the placed Porsches, even if some 200km (125 miles) behind the leading 904 GTS of Buchet and Ligier. It should be noted that all of the five 904s finished the race.

Porsche no. 30. Type 904/8, Prototype class, entered by Porsche System and driven by Davis and Mitter. It retired in the 20th hour, after being in 16th place in the preceding hour.

Bonnier and Hill, usually the top Porsche drivers, were in a Ferrari so Davis and Mitter were at the wheel of this, the second of the prototype 8-cylinder cars. It was in second place in the middle of the night, but clutch trouble forced it to retire in the 20th hour after falling further down the field.

Porsche no. 29. Type 904/8, Prototype class, entered by Porsche System and driven by Barth and Linge. It retired in the 11th hour, after being in eighth place in the preceding hour.

At 2.30 in the morning Porsche no. 29 had been at the top of the Index of Performance. However, at the exit from the Tertre Rouge S-bend, Linge at the wheel, the Porsche's clutch packed up, leaving the Ferrari of the winners-to-be to go to the top of its class. It should be noted that this Porsche prototype was timed on the Hunaudières straight at 282km/h (175mph).

Race no.	Type Model	Engine position	Number of cylinders	Capacity in cc	Bore & stroke in mm	Valve operation	Cooling	Induction	Brakes	Transmission	Body material	Weight in kg (lb)
29	904/8	Rear	Flat-8	1981	76 x 54.6	2 ohc	air	4 Weber	discs	Porsche 5+R	polyester	757 (1669)
30	904/8	Rear	Flat-8	1981	76 x 54.6	2 ohc	air	4 Weber	discs	Porsche 5+R	polyester	788 (1737)
31	904GTS	Rear	Flat-4	1967	92 x 74	2 ohc	air	2 Weber	discs	Porsche 5+R	polyester	771 (1700)
32	904GTS	Rear	Flat-4	1967	92 x 74	2 ohc	air	2 Weber	discs	Porsche 5+R	polyester	783 (1726)
33	904GTS	Rear	Flat-4	1967	92 x 74	2 ohc	air	2 Weber	discs	Porsche 5+R	polyester	788 (1737)
34	904GTS	Rear	Flat-4	1967	92 x 74	2 ohc	air	2 Weber	discs	Porsche 5+R	polyester	780 (1720)
35	904GTS	Rear	Flat-4	1967	92 x 74	2 ohc	air	2 Weber	discs	Porsche 5+R	polyester	722 (1702)

1965

Seven Porsches start, two finish

The contest at the top between Ford and Ferrari was well and truly on, but none of the American cars was to be amongst the leaders at the finish: three Ferraris took the first three places, in front of two Porsches.

The arrival of the 6-cylinder units reinforced the line-up of Porsche engines: one 8-cylinder, two 6-cylinder and four 4-cylinder cars were at the start. (Although, it would be a long time before another Porsche 4-cylinder engine took part in Le Mans).

It was the 275LM Ferrari of Gregory and Rindt that won on distance, covering 4677.11km (2906.22 miles) at an average of 194.88km/h (121.09mph).

Porsche no. 32. Type 904/6 (engine no. 901-06), Prototype class entered by Porsche System and driven by Linge and Nöcker. It came fourth in distance, covering 4507.50km (2800.83 miles) in 24 hours at an average of 187.81km/h (116.70mph) and first in the Index of Performance.

This Porsche victory in the Index of Performance, was due in part to the withdrawal of the Alpines that had dominated this competition previously. No one at Stuttgart had expected this victory and it was therefore given very little publicity.

Porsche no. 36. Type 904 GTS (engine no. P.99158), GT class, entered by Porsche System and driven by Koch and Fischaber. It came fifth in distance, covering 4366.66 km (2711.31 miles) in 24 hours at an average of 181.94 km/h (113.05mph), and third in the Index of Performance.

The only works GTS entered, this car completed the Porsche roll of honour by carrying off the Index of Efficiency ahead of the Dumay-Gosselin Ferrari, and fifth place overall, in front of the Ferraris and a Cobra — all with distinctly mightier engines ...

Porsche no. 35. Type 904/6 (chassis no. 904/08), Prototype class entered by Porsche System and driven by Klass and Glemser. It retired in the 15th hour, after being in 11th place in the preceding hour. It was at 7.40am that a valve gave out, forcing retirement and leaving the company's hopes pinned on the surviving 6-cylinder car, which finished in fourth place overall.

Porsche no. 37. Type 904 GTS (engine no. P.99014), GT class, entered by Veuillet and driven by Buchet and Ben Pon. It retired in the 16th hour, after being in 10th place in the preceding hour. The end for no. 37 came at 8.40 on Sunday morning, with a broken connecting rod.

Porsche no. 33. Type 904/8 (engine no. 77-105), Prototype class entered by Porsche System and driven by Davis and Mitter. It retired in the fourth hour, after being in 41st place in the preceding hour. This, the only 8-cylinder car entered, damaged its clutch at 6.30 in the evening. It had a difficult race and did not live up to the hopes placed on it. In practice, Davis and Mitter had achieved a 3m 59.4s lap, the best time after the Fords, Ferraris and a Cobra.

Porsche no. 38. Type 904 GTS (engine no. P.99033), GT class, entered by 'Franc' and driven by 'Franc' and Kerguen. It retired in the eighth hour, after being in 17th place in the preceding hour. This team was obliged to abandon the race when a leak in the tank left the car without fuel.

Porsche no. 62. Type 904 GTS (engine no. P.9908), GT class, entered by C. Poirot and driven by Stommelen and Poirot. It retired in the second hour, after being in 30th place in the preceding hour. The car had problems with a damaged gearbox.

Race no.	Type Model	Engine position	Number of cylinders	Capacity in cc	Bore & stroke in mm	Valve operation	Cooling	Induction	Brakes	Transmission	Body material	Weight in kg (lb)
32	904/6	Rear	Flat-6	1990	80 x 66	2 ohc	air	2 Weber	discs	Porsche 5+R	polyester	711 (1700)
33	904/8	Rear	Flat-8	1984.5	76 x 54	2 ohc	air	2 Weber	discs	Porsche 5+R	polyester	756 (1667)
35	904/6	Rear	Flat-6	1990	80 x 66	2 ohc	air	2 Weber	discs	Porsche 5+R	polyester	740 (1631)
36	904GTS	Rear	Flat-4	1967.7	92 x 74	2 ohc	air	2 Weber	discs	Porsche 5+R	polyester	783 (1726)
37	904GTS	Rear	Flat-4	1967.7	92 x 74	2 ohc	air	2 Weber	discs	Porsche 5+R	polyester	796 (1755)
38	904GTS	Rear	Flat-4	1967.7	92 x 74	2 ohc	air	2 Weber	discs	Porsche 5+R	polyester	814 (1795)
62	904GTS	Rear	Flat-4	1967.7	92 x 74	2 ohc	air	2 Weber	discs	Porsche 5+R	polyester	775 (1709)

1966

Seven Porsches start, five finish

In a vigorous response to the new rules, Porsche fielded its fleet of short-tailed 906s (fulfilling the new Sports homologation criteria with 50 examples manufactured) and long-tails (for the Prototype category). The 906s differed radically from the 904s in having a spaceframe construction instead of the conventional chassis type of their predecessors.

Fuel-injection made its appearance on the 6-cylinder racers, giving an extra 10bhp, and Porsche achieved a splendidly grouped result a few lengths behind the winners, McLaren and Amon, who ushered in the Ford era at Le Mans at an average of 201.79km/h (125.39mph), covering 4843.09km (3009.35 miles).

Porsche no. 30. Type 906 long-tail (chassis no. 906-153), Prototype class, entered by Porsche System and driven by Siffert and Davis. It was placed fourth in distance, covering 4562.13km (2834.77 miles) at an average of 190.08km/h (118.11mph). It was also first in the Index of Performance and eighth in the Index of Efficiency.

One of three Porsches to come top in the Index of Performance, no. 30 also took the 2-litre class and capped these successes with fourth place overall: a fine performance by a picked team in a car representing the very forefront of technological progress. Note that this long-tail 906 had fuel-injection. When would the 8-cylinder be similarly equipped – for an outright win?

Porsche no. 31. Type 906 long-tail (chassis no. 906-143), Prototype class, entered by Porsche System and driven by Hermann and Linge. It came fifth in distance, covering 4548.37km (2826.22 miles) in 24 hours at an average of 189.51km/h (117.41mph). It was also second in the Index of Performance and ninth in the Index of Efficiency.

This car was basically the same as the Siffert-Davis car, but fitted with carburettors. It added to the Porsche roll of honour after an uneventful race.

Porsche no. 32. Type 906 long-tail (chassis no. 906-152), Prototype class, entered by Porsche System and driven by Schutz and de Klerk. It came sixth in distance, covering 4534.93km (2817.87 miles) at an average 188.95km/h (117.41mph). It was also fourth in the Index of Performance and 10th in the Index of Efficiency. It was the second fuel-injection Porsche in the race.

Porsche no. 33. Type 906 (chassis no. 906-112), entered by Porsche System and driven by Gregg and Axelsson. It retired in the 24th hour, after being in seventh place in the preceding hour. This was the last retirement from the event, a few minutes from the finish. This American-Swedish combination had to retire with rocker and valve trouble. Thanks to its good position, dearly gained, it was able to secure a place in the massed Porsche 906 finish.

Porsche no. 35. Type 911 (engine no. 903-355), GT class, entered by Jacques Dewez and driven by Kerguen and 'Franc'. It came 14th in the distance classification, covering 3821.53km (2374.58 miles) in 24 hours at an average of 159.23km/h (98.94mph), and 12th in the Index of Performance.

This was the first 911 entered in the Le Mans 24 Hours. It turned in a good performance — it at least completed the event. As promised before the start, this 911 was put up for sale after the race.

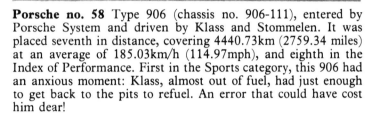

Porsche no. 58 Type 906 (chassis no. 906-111), entered by Porsche System and driven by Klass and Stommelen. It was placed seventh in distance, covering 4440.73km (2759.34 miles) at an average of 185.03km/h (114.97mph), and eighth in the Index of Performance. First in the Sports category, this 906 had an anxious moment: Klass, almost out of fuel, had just enough to get back to the pits to refuel. An error that could have cost him dear!

Porsche no. 34. Type 906 (chassis no. 906-104), driven by Buchet and Koch. It retired in the ninth hour, after being in 18th place in the preceding hour. Robert Buchet ran into the barriers at the top of the Dunlop curve as it began to rain. Fortunately Buchet got out unharmed but the car was destroyed.

Race no.	Type Model	Engine position	Number of cylinders	Capacity in cc	Bore & stroke in mm	Valve operation	Cooling	Induction	Brakes	Transmission	Body material	Weight in kg (lb)
30	906L	Rear	Flat-6	1990	80 x 66	ohc	air	injection	discs	Porsche 5 + R	polyester	–
31	906L	Rear	Flat-6	1990	80 x 66	ohc	air	2 Weber	discs	Porsche 5 + R	polyester	–
32	906L	Rear	Flat-6	1990	80 x 66	ohc	air	injection	discs	Porsche 5 + R	polyester	–
33	906L	Rear	Flat-6	1990	80 x 66	ohc	air	2 Weber	discs	Porsche 5 + R	polyester	–
34	906	Rear	Flat-6	1990	80 x 66	ohc	air	2 Weber	discs	Porsche 5 + R	polyester	–
35	911	Rear	Flat-6	1990	80 x 66	ohc	air	2 Weber	discs	Porsche 5 + R	steel	–
58	906	Rear	Flat-6	1990	80 x 66	ohc	air	2 Weber	discs	Porsche 5 + R	polyester	–

1967

Ten Porsches start, five finish

There were no Porsche 8-cylinder cars at Le Mans this year. The Stuttgart marque was not confident enough in this engine to venture it again in such a long event; it was the 6-cylinder engines with fuel-injection that carried the marque's hopes. Innovations were the 910, a derivative of the 'Bergspyder' provided with a roof, and the 907, a new long-tail car. It was announced before the race that the 907 exceeded 300km/h (185mph) — a speed it did not attain during the event.

This year was distinguished above all by the Ford-Ferrari duel, with seven cars in each team. In the end it was a Ford that won, at an average 218.03km/h (135.48mph), establishing the Americans Gurney and Foyt, who in 24 hours had covered a total of 5232.90km (3251.57 miles) — a new record.

Porsche no. 41. Type 907 (chassis no. 907-004), Prototype class, entered by Porsche System and driven by Siffert and Herrman. It was placed fifth on distance, covering 4830.65km (3002.62 miles) in 24 hours at an average of 201.27km/h (125.06mph), and first in the Index of Performance.

Like Rindt, Siffert and Hermann made a thundering start. However, with Rindt out after over-revving his car's engine, this team kept up the pressure, eating up places and benefiting from retirements throughout the race and finally taking the Index of Performance, the 2-litre class and exceeding an average 200 km/h (125mph) for the first time in a Porsche!

Porsche no. 37. Type 906 (chassis no. 906-154), entered by Porsche System and driven by Elford and Ben Pon. It came seventh in distance, covering 4409.45km (2739.90 miles) in 24 hours at an average 183.72km/h (114.16mph) and 10th in the Index of Performance. This car could have finished in a better position if ignition trouble had not slowed it down. Nevertheless it won the Sports category — from Porsche no. 66 and an Abarth.

Porsche no. 38. Type 901, Prototype class, entered by Porsche System and driven by Stommelen and Neerpasch. It was placed sixth in distance, covering 4735.90km (2942.75 miles) in 24 hours at an average of 197.32km/h (122.61mph), and third in the Index of Performance.

An uneventful race for the second 910, which finished with an average close to the 200km/h (125mph) mark. It could certainly have passed this threshold if it had engaged in more duelling at the start.

Porsche no. 66. Type 906, driven by Poirot and Koch. It was placed eighth in the distance classification, covering 4328.69km (2689.72 miles) in 24 hours at an average of 180.36km/h (112.07 mph), and 12th in the Index of Performance. From the early hours of the morning, this team had to nurse its car's clutch; the problem allowing Porsche no. 37 to deprive it of seventh place.

Porsche no. 42. Type 911S, GT class, entered by Veuillet and driven by Buchet and Linge. It was placed 14th on distance, covering 4158.09km (2583.71 miles) in 24 hours at an average of 173.25km/h (107.65mph) and 14th in the Index of Performance. This car also achieved second place in the GT category (behind a 3.3-litre Ferrari 275GTB), after a race resembling that of the renowned timekeeper Dutray.

Porsche no. 40. Type 907 (chassis no. 907-003), Prototype class, entered by Porsche System and driven by Rindt and Mitter. It retired in the seventh hour, after being in 26th place in the preceding hour. Despite the small capacity of his car's engine (2-litres), the fiery Jochen Rindt went after the Fords and Ferraris despite their bigger power units.

Porsche no. 67. Type 911S, GT class, entered by Boutin and driven by Boutin and Sanson. An illegal replenishment of lubricating oil brought about the disqualification of this privately-entered Porsche in the 11th hour, after it had been in 28th place in the preceding hour. This topping up took place at the end of 23 laps instead of the authorized 25: a regrettable mistake.

Porsche no. 39. Type 901 (chassis no. 907-005), Prototype class, entered by Porsche System and driven by Buzzetta and Schutz. It retired in the sixth hour, after being in 24th place in the preceding hour. Retirement was necessary, when towards 10.00pm the oil pressure fell irreparably.

Porsche no. 60. Type 911S, GT class, entered by Farjon, driven by Wicky and Farjon. It retired in the 11th hour, with a burned-out piston, after being in 29th place in the preceding hour.

Porsche no. 43. Type 911S (engine no. 961-778), GT class, entered by Jacques Dewez and driven by 'Franc' and Fischaber. It retired in the first hour after the 'Franc'-Fischaber team wrecked their clutch on the starting line, making them a rather inglorious first on the casualty list!

Race no.	Type Model	Engine position	Number of cylinders	Capacity in cc	Bore & stroke in mm	Valve operation	Cooling	Induction	Brakes	Transmission	Body material	Weight in kg (lb)
37	906	Rear	Flat-6	1990	80 x 66	ohc	air	2 Weber	discs	Porsche 5+R	polyester	–
38	910	Rear	Flat-6	1990	80 x 66	ohc	air	injection	discs	Porsche 5+R	polyester	–
39	910	Rear	Flat-6	1990	80 x 66	ohc	air	injection	discs	Porsche 5+R	polyester	–
40	907	Rear	Flat-6	1990	80 x 66	ohc	air	injection	discs	Porsche 5+R	polyester	–
41	907	Rear	Flat-6	1990	80 x 66	ohc	air	injection	discs	Porsche 5+R	polyester	600 (1323)
42	911S	Rear	Flat-6	1990	80 x 66	ohc	air	2 Weber	discs	Porsche 5+R	steel	–
43	911S	Rear	Flat-6	1990	80 x 66	ohc	air	2 Weber	discs	Porsche 5+R	steel	–
60	911S	Rear	Flat-6	1990	80 x 66	ohc	air	2 Weber	discs	Porsche 5+R	steel	–
66	906	Rear	Flat-6	1990	80 x 66	ohc	air	2 Weber	discs	Porsche 5+R	polyester	–
67	911S	Rear	Flat-6	1990	80 x 66	ohc	air	2 Weber	discs	Porsche 5+R	steel	–

1968

Thirteen Porsches start, four finish

This was a year of great hopes vested in new cars conforming to the new rules for Prototypes (less than 3-litres) and Sports Racing cars (less than 5-litres). There was a record Porsche entry: works 908s, semi-private 907s and private customers making up this remarkable number with a few 911s. There was dismay in the pits over the various problems that put nine cars out of the event. However, one survivor took second place overall behind the Ford of Pedro Rodriguez and Lucien Bianchi, which covered 4452.88km (2766.89 miles) at an average of 185.53km/h (115.28mph)

Unusually, the Le Mans 24 Hours was run in September in 1968, on account of the political events of May of that year.

Porsche no. 66. Type 907 (chassis no. 907-003), Sports/Prototype class entered by the Swiss Squadra Tartaruga and driven by Spoerry and Steinemann. It was second in distance, covering 4378.72km (2720.81 miles) in 24 hours at an average of 182.44km/h (113.36mph). It was also third in the Index of Performance and ninth in the Index of Efficiency. Porsche was 'saved' by the Swiss team and their redoubtable 907. This fantastic, and unexpected, second place was some consolation for von Hanstein who had been dreaming of outright victory this year. Steinemann spinning the car round twice on the Hunaudières straight and a cracked brake disc were the only snags in this car's very consistent race. It also won the Sports/Prototype category.

Porsche no. 33. Type 908 (chassis no. 908-013), Sports/Prototype class, entered by Porsche System and driven by Stommelen and Neerpasch. It was placed third in the distance classification, covering 4366.22km (2713.04 miles) in 24 hours at an average of 181.92km/h (113.04mph). It was also eighth in the Index of Performance and ninth in the Index of Efficiency.

Stommelen at the wheel of this car, took the lap record with a time of 3m 38.1s, which is 222.32km/h (138.14mph). At the beginning of the race trouble with the fanbelt had impeded the car's progress considerably. Subsequently a very hard race prevented this car from giving its best. It should be pointed out that the four Porsche 908s were fitted with movable aerofoils supported by the suspension, giving them greater stability on the bends and better straight-line braking.

Porsche no. 43. Type 911s, GT class, entered by Gaban and driven by Gaban and Vanderschriek. It came 12th in distance, covering 3783.85km (2351.17 miles) in 24 hours, at an average of 157.66km/h (97.96mph), and 15th in the Index of Performance. This Belgian team was placed first in the category.

Porsche no. 64. Type 911T, GT class, entered by Laurent and driven by Laurent and Ogier. It was placed 13th in the distance classification, covering 3710.94km (2305.87 miles) in 24 hours at an average 154.62km/h (96.07mph), and 14th in the Index of Performance. The car also achieved 2nd in the GT category. behind Porsche 911, no. 43.

Porsche no. 44. Type 911S, GT class, entered by Veuillet and driven by Chasseuil and Ballot Lena. It retired in the 24th hour, after being in 12th place in the preceding hour. This French team had to give up after 23 hours 45 minutes and only two laps from the end, because of engine failure.

Porsche no. 45. Type 910 (chassis no. 910-007), Sports/Prototype class, entered by Hanrioud, driven by Hanrioud and Wicky. It retired in the 23rd hour, after being in 17th place in the preceding hour.

A damaged valve rocker slowed this car down. On the following day, within view of the finish, the same trouble recurred forcing the team to withdraw.

Porsche no. 42. Type 906 entered by Poirot, driven by Poirot and Maublanc. It was disqualified in the 19th hour, after being in 19th place in the preceding hour. Christian Poirot was forced to make use of an escape road and, according to the rules, he should have stopped at the pits the next time round. He did not do so and this forgetfulness caused the disqualification of this French team.

Porsche no. 35. Type 907, Sports/Prototype class, entered by Soler Roig and driven by Soler Roig and Lins. It retired in the 12th hour, after being in 21st place in the preceding hour. This Hispano-Austrian team was very unlucky. When their car was lying in third place a valve rocker broke, entailing lengthy repairs and then retirement.

Porsche no. 67. Type 907 (chassis no. 907-706), Sports/Prototype class, entered by Farjon/Tours ORTF and driven by Buchet and Linge. It was disqualified in the ninth hour after being in 20th place in the preceding hour. Buchet-Linge had to change a front wheel, but then the starter broke and before it could be replaced this had incurred the disqualification.

Porsche no. 32. Type 908 (chassis no. 908-012), Sports/Prototype class, entered by Porsche System and driven by Mitter and Elford. A series of troubles — overheated engine, clutch problems — slowed this Porsche down, but it was an alternator fault that finally stopped it. The mechanics changed this item but as replacement was forbidden by the rules, the car was disqualified in the 9th hour, after being in 14th place.

Porsche no. 31. Type 908 (chassis no. 908-016), Sports/Prototype class entered by Porsche System and driven by Siffert and Herrmann. It withdrew in the fifth hour, after being in second place in the preceding hour.

About 330km/h (205mph) was the top speed of this Porsche in which Siffert contended for first place — a position he held for the first three hours of the event until transmission trouble put a stop to his exploits: he was two laps in the lead ...

Porsche no. 34. Type 908, (chassis no. 908-015), Sports/Prototype class entered by Porsche System and driven by Buzetta and Patrick. It retired in the 9th hour, after being in 14th place in the preceding hour. This team was leading when the first troubles occurred. The 8-cylinder engine began to vibrate badly. This damaged the alternator, breaking its mounting and forcing retirement.

Porsche no. 60. Type 911, GT class, entered by Wicky Racing Team and driven by Meier and de Mortement. It retired in the third hour, after being in 38th place in the preceding hour. Mortement was driving when the car left the track at the Terte Rouge and was too badly damaged to continue.

Race no.	Type Model	Engine position	Number of cylinders	Capacity in cc	Bore & stroke in mm	Valve operation	Cooling	Induction	Brakes	Transmission	Body material	Weight in kg (lb)
31	908	Rear	Flat-8	2996	85 x 66	ohc	air	injection	discs	Porsche 6+R	polyester	710 (1565)
32	908	Rear	Flat-8	2996	85 x 66	ohc	air	injection	discs	Porsche 6+R	polyester	710 (1565)
33	908	Rear	Flat-8	2996	85 x 66	ohc	air	injection	discs	Porsche 6+R	polyster	710 (1565)
34	908	Rear	Flat-8	2996	85 x 66	ohc	air	injection	discs	Porsche 6+R	polyester	710 (1565)
35	907	Rear	Flat-8	2996	80 x 54.6	ohc	air	injection	discs	Porsche 5+R	polyester	–
42	906	Rear	Flat-6	1991	80 x 66	ohc	air	2 Weber	discs	Porsche 5+R	polyester	625 (1378)
43	911S	Rear	Flat-6	1991	80 x 66	ohc	air	2 Weber	discs	Porsche 5+R	steel	925 (2039)
44	911S	Rear	Flat-6	1991	80 x 66	ohc	air	2 Weber	discs	Porsche 5+R	steel	925 (2039)
45	910	Rear	Flat-6	1991	80 x 66	ohc	air	injection	discs	Porsche 5+R	polyester	575 (1268)
60	911T	Rear	Flat-6	1991	80 x 66	ohc	air	2 Weber	discs	Porsche 5+R	steel	925 (2039)
64	911T	Rear	Flat-6	1991	80 x 66	ohc	air	2 Weber	discs	Porsche 5+R	steel	925 (2039)
66	907	Rear	Flat-6	1991	80 x 66	ohc	air	injection	discs	Porsche 5+R	polyester	–
67	907	Rear	Flat-8	2195	80 x 54.6	ohc	air	injection	discs	Porsche 5+R	polyester	712 (1570)

1969

Sixteen Porsches start, six finish

This year saw the appearance of the famous Porsche 917, Stuttgart's response to the FIA's new rules for the Sports Racing category, and also a challenge to Ferrari who had similarly produced a car to shine in this classification. Four 917s took part in the practice runs but only three started the event. These cars developed some 580bhp, had movable aerofoils mounted on the suspension, and much was expected of them. Their 12-cylinder, 4.5-litre engines retained many of the mechanical parts of the 908 units. In practice Stommelen lapped in 3m 22.9s, a new record at an average of 238.97km/h (148.49mph): which meant a top speed of about 360km/h (224mph) on the Hunaudières straight! But despite these outstanding performances, it was the Ickx-Olivier Ford that won on distance, covering 4998km (3105.61 miles) at 208.25km/h (129.40mph).

Porsche no. 64. Type 908 long-tail (chassis no. 908-031), Sports/Prototype class, entered by Porsche System and driven by Herrman and Larrousse. It was placed second in distance, covering 4997.88km (3105.53 miles) in 24 hours at an average of 208.24km/h (129.39mph), and second in the Index of Performance.

A cracked axle bearing slowed this Porsche 908, which was in second place in the last three hours. The tussle that developed between Herrmann and Ickx for first place has gone down in the annals of motor racing history. After 13 hours, just 2 seconds separated the Porsche and the Ford. It was a real Grand Prix type finale that made those present tremble for the machines, already battered by more than 20 hours of racing. The Porsche had the better acceleration but the Ford (and Ickx) went round the bends better. The two cars overtook each other many times during the last hour, providing a remarkable spectacle and racing neck-and-neck at the extreme limit of machine and driver. There was a brilliant last lap with the spectators on their feet, cheering and waving. Ickx won, but this was no discredit to Herrmann. It was a great Le Mans.

Porsche no. 39. Type 910 (chassis no. 910-006), Sports/Prototype class, entered by Poirot and driven by Poirot and Maublanc. It was placed ninth in distance, covering 4191.41km (2604.42 miles) in 24 hours at an average 174.64km/h (108.51mph), and ninth in the Index of Performance. Exhaust problems affected the progress of this second 910. It finished nevertheless as the first French team home, and first in the 2-litre class.

Porsche no. 41. Type 911S, GT class, entered by Gaban and driven by Gaban and Deprez. It was classed 10th on distance, covering 4120.56km (2560.39 miles) in 24 hours at an average of 171.69km/h (106.68mph). It was also 10th in the Index of Performance and 7th in the Index of Efficiency. This car finished first of the GTs, in front of three other Porsches, after a consistent race that took it from 32nd place in the first hour to 10th at the finish.

Porsche no. 67. Type 911S, GT class, entered by Farjon and driven by Farjon and Dechaumel. It was placed 14th in distance, covering 3845.47km (2389.46 miles) in 24 hours at an average of 160.22km/h (99.56mph), and 14th in the Index of Performance. Last of the Porsches that finished, it at least secured a placing.

Porsche no. 40. Type 911T, GT class, entered by Veuillet, driven by Ballot Lena and Chasseuil. It was 11th in distance, covering 4052.58km (2518.15 miles) in 24 hours at an average of 168.85km/h (104.92mph). It also came 12th in the Index of Performance and 5th equal in the Index of Efficiency. This car finished second in the GT class, behind the Gaban-Deprez car; it had an uneventful race.

Porsche no. 22. Type 908 long-tail, Sports/Prototype class (chassis no. 908-029), entered by Porsche System and driven by Lins and Kauhsen. It retired in the 22nd hour after being in sixth place in the preceding hour. The Lins-Kauhsen 908 followed the Porsche of the leaders Elford and Attwood, until it retired with gearbox trouble.

Porsche no. 44. Type 911T, GT class, entered by Laurent and driven by Laurent and Marche. It was placed 13th in distance, covering 3864km (2400.97 miles) in 24 hours at an average of 161.km/h (100mph). It also came 13th in the Index of Performance and 9th in the Index of Efficiency.

Porsche no. 12. Type 917 long-tail (chassis no. 917-008), entered by Porsche System and driven by Elford and Attwood. It retired in the 21st hour after being in first place.

Elford was first from the fourth hour, the position that car held until the 21st hour. Attwood, who was then at the wheel, stopped to adjust the clutch which had been giving him bother: at the time he had a four-lap lead over the Ickx-Olivier Ford. When Attwood restarted the mechanics knew that their makeshift repair would not last. His lead melted away and the car returned to the pits to retire. When the mechanics pushed it over the line they were given an ovation by the Le Mans spectators.

Porsche no. 66. Type 911T, GT class, entered by Egreteaud and driven by Egreteaud and Lopez. It retired in the 20th hour, after being in 14th place in the preceding hour. Lopez was at the wheel when the Porsche left the track sustaining considerable damage.

Porsche no. 63. Type 911T, GT class, entered by Martin and driven by Mazzia and Mauroy. It retired in the 16th hour with bearing problems in the gearbox, after being in 22nd place in the preceding hour.

Porsche no. 14. Type 917 long-tail (chassis no. 917-007) entered by Porsche System and driven by Stommelen and Ahrens. It retired in the 15th hour after being in 23rd place in the preceding hour.

Stommelen, who drove at the start, ended the first lap with a considerable lead which he held on to, finishing the first hour in front. Unfortunately, an engine oil leak slowed him down. Clutch problems then put him out completely, when the Porsche had dropped back to the bottom of its classification.

Porsche no. 23. Type 908 long-tail (chassis no. 908-030), Sports/Prototype class, entered by Porsche System and driven by Schutz and Mitter. It retired in the 14th hour after being in third place in the preceding hour.

Udo Schutz was at the wheel when, about halfway through the race, he was overtaken by Larrousse: the latter having sorted out his bearing problems. Affronted, Schutz endeavoured to pass Porsche no. 14 and left the track on the bend at Hunaudières in the attempt. The car caught fire after its driver had been pulled clear. This 'retirement' certainly cost the team a creditable placing.

Porsche no. 20. Type 908 Spyder (chassis no. 908-028), Sports/Prototype class, entered by Hart Ski Racing and driven by Siffert and Redman. It retired in the sixth hour after being in 33rd place in the preceding hour. After a thundering start by Siffert, who was matching the Porsche 917s and was in first place at the pit stops, the 908 Spyder had to retire when an oil pipe to the gearbox broke.

Porsche no. 60. Type 910, Sports/Prototype class, driven by Mortemart and Mésange. It retired in the second hour after being in 42nd place in the preceding hour. This team had no chance of continuing when a connecting rod decided to go its own way, early in the race.

Porsche no. 42. Type 911T, GT class, entered by Wicky Racing Team and driven by Wicky and Berney. It retired in the fourth hour with a cracked piston after being in 37th place in the preceding hour.

Porsche no. 10. Type 917 short-tail (chassis no. 917-005), entered by John Woolfe Racing and driven by Woolfe and Linge.

Many will remember the dramatic accident that cost the life of John Woolfe on the first lap of the race. The car left the track at Maison Blanche and John Woolfe was killed. A spate of retirements followed, notably that of Amon whose Ferrari went out after puncturing its tyres on the debris of the Woolfe-Linge 917 strewn across the track.

Race no.	Type Model	Engine position	Number of cylinders	Capacity in cc	Bore & stroke in mm	Valve operation	Cooling	Induction	Brakes	Transmission	Body material	Weight in kg (lb)
10	917	Rear	Flat-12	4494	85 x 66	ohc	air	injection	discs	Porsche 5+R	polyester	944 (2081)
12	917L	Rear	Flat-12	4494	85 x 66	ohc	air	injection	discs	Porsche 5+R	polyester	948 (2090)
14	917L	Rear	Flat-12	4494	85 x 66	ohc	air	injection	discs	Porsche 5+R	polyester	952 (2099)
20	908S	Rear	Flat-8	2996	85 x 66	ohc	air	injection	discs	Porsche 5+R	polyester	746 (1645)
22	908L	Rear	Flat-8	2996	85 x 66	ohc	air	injection	discs	Porsche 5+R	polyester	712 (1570)
23	908	Rear	Flat-8	2996	85 x 66	ohc	air	injection	discs	Porsche 5+R	polyester	746 (1645)
39	910	Rear	Flat-6	1991	80 x 66	ohc	air	injection	discs	Porsche 5+R	polyester	645 (1422)
40	911T	Rear	Flat-6	1991	80 x 66	ohc	air	2 Weber	discs	Porsche 5+R	steel	1012 (2231)
41	911S	Rear	Flat-6	1991	80 x 66	ohc	air	2 Weber	discs	Porsche 5+R	steel	1012 (2231)
42	911T	Rear	Flat-6	1991	80 x 66	ohc	air	2 Weber	discs	Porsche 5+R	steel	994 (2191)
44	911T	Rear	Flat-6	1991	80 x 66	ohc	air	2 Weber	discs	Porsche 5+R	steel	1010 (2227)
60	910	Rear	Flat-6	1991	80 x 66	ohc	air	injection	discs	Porsche 5+R	polyester	652 (1437)
63	911T	Rear	Flat-6	1991	80 x 66	ohc	air	2 Weber	discs	Porsche 5+R	steel	1014 (2235)
64	908L	Rear	Flat-8	2996	85 x 66	ohc	air	injection	discs	Porsche 5+R	polyester	739 (1629)
66	911T	Rear	Flat-6	1991	80 x 66	ohc	air	2 Weber	discs	Porsche 5+R	steel	997 (2198)
67	911S	Rear	Flat-6	1991	80 x 66	ohc	air	2 Weber	discs	Porsche 5+R	steel	1096 (2416)

1970

Twenty-four Porsches start, twelve finish, five are placed

It had taken Porsche twenty years to win the distance category at Le Mans. This was a somewhat bitter victory, however, because of the way in which it was gained: potential winners were eliminated early on when they ran off the track; the weather was dreadful, torrents of rain falling on the course; and the crowd became bored with a most uninteresting race. John Wyer entered three short-tail 917s, not so fast as, but more stable than, the long-tails; two of them had the 5-litre engine. Porsche fielded two 917s and Martini Racing entered one. But whatever the circumstances, there was a whole heap of honours for Porsche: first place in distance, in the Index of Performance, the Index of Efficiency, in the GT, Sports and Prototype groups as well as in all the classes, including the lap record!

Porsche no. 23. Type 917 (chassis no. 917-023), entered by Porsche Konstruktionen and driven by Herrmann and Attwood. It was placed first in the distance classification, covering 4607.81km (2863.16 miles) in 24 hours at an average 191.99km/h (119.29mph). It was also second in the Index of Performance and fourth in the Index of Efficiency.

Thought to be the least good of the 917s, this car proved the best. It was credited with the worst time in the trials (3m 32.6s), but this did not prevent it triumphing after its Anglo-German team had driven a very consistent race. Lying ninth in the first hour, it was then in first place from the eleventh hour to the finish.

Porsche no. 3. Type 917 long-tail (chassis no. 917-043), entered by Martini Racing and driven by Larrousse and Kauhsen. It came second in distance, covering 4541.95km (2822.23 miles) in 24 hours at an average of 189.24km/h (117.59mph). It also came third in the Index of Performance and first in the Index of Efficiency.

An excellent second place overall for this Franco-German team. Although entered by Martini, it was really a Porsche works car, comparable to the Elford-Ahrens machine. The ignition caused a few worries when the rain started to fall: the engine was not responding to demand altogether as it should. This car did not produce quite what might have been expected of it, considering that it achieved 3m 30.8s in practice – more than 10s better than the winning 917's best practice time.

Porsche no. 27. Type 908 (chassis no. 908-050), Sports/Prototype class, entered by Martini Racing Team and driven by Lins and Marko. It came third in distance, covering 4502.78km (2797.89 miles)) in 24 hours at an average of 187.61km/h (116.57mph). It was also first in the Index of Performance and third in the Index Efficiency.

First in the Sports/Prototype category, first in the Index of Performance and first in the 3-litre class: these were the titles carried off by this very light – 648kg (1429lb) – and very streamlined 908 Spyder.

Porsche no. 40. Type 914/6, GTS class, entered by Sonauto and driven by Chasseuil and Ballot Lena. It came sixth in distance, covering 3834.26km (2382.50 miles) in 24 hours at an average of 159.76km/h (99.27mph). It was also fourth in the Index of Performance and second in the Index of Efficiency. For a first outing, the 914/6 came through the pitfalls of le Mans very well. After a very consistent race it took the first place in the GT group – from Greder's Corvette. It also won the 2-litre class.

Porsche no. 47. Type 911S, GTS class, entered by the Luxemburg team and driven by Koob and Kremer. It came seventh in the distance classification, covering 3790.63km (2355.38 miles) in 24 hours at an average 157.94km/h (98.14mph). It was also sixth in the Index of Performance and fifth in the Index of Efficiency. Koob and Kremer drove a very regular race in the last Porsche to be placed, outstripping the other 911s, which did not cover a sufficient distance to qualify for a position.

Porsche no. 29. Type 908/2 (chassis no. 908-013), Sports/Prototype class, entered by Solar Production and driven by Linge and Williams. This 908 entered by the late Steve McQueen did not cover enough distance to be placed, but did achieve some superb views of Le Mans: it was fitted with three cameras which provided footage for the film *Le Mans*, in which the famous American actor played the part of a racing driver.

Porsche no. 42. Type 911T, GTS class, entered by Wicky Racing Team and driven by Verrier and Garant. It did not succeed in covering a sufficient distance for a placing.

Porsche no. 64. Type 911S (engine no. 13443), GTS class, entered by Halot and driven by Sage and Greub. This car finished, but without covering enough distance to be placed.

Porsche no. 45. Type 911S (chassis no. 911-02), GTS class, entered by Laurent and driven by Laurent and Marche. It was not placed as it did not cover a sufficient distance.

Porsche no. 66. Type 911S (engine no. 12627), GTS class, entered by Touroul and driven by Swietlik and Lagniez. It was unplaced at the end of the 24 hours, which it completed, as the distance it covered was insufficient.

Porsche no. 67. Type 911S, GTS class, entered by Dechaumel and driven by Parot and Dechaumel. It was not placed, not having covered the minimum distance required.

Porsche no. 62. Type 911S, GTS class, entered by Mazzia and driven by Mauroy and Mazzia. It finished, but did not cover sufficient distance for a place.

Porsche no. 65. Type 911S, GTS class, entered by Hart Ski Racing and driven by Haldi and Blank. It retired in the 16th hour with gearbox trouble, after being in 21st place in the preceding hour.

Porsche no. 25. Type 917 long-tail (chassis no. 917-042), entered by Porsche Konstruktionen and driven by Elford and Ahrens. It retired in the 17th hour, after being in fourth place in the preceding hour. It was this team that achieved the best time in practice – 3m 19.8s – thanks to the streamlined long-tail shape of the car.

Elford, given the choice, decided to make the start in the machine in which he had clocked this tremendous time – 0.12s ahead of Giunti's Ferrari. At the end of the first hour of the race this 917 was in first place, a position it lost to Siffert. Unfortunately its engine could not stand up to the punishment of the speeds attained – 331km/h (206mph) – and to more than 16 hours of thundering round the course.

Porsche no. 61. Type 907 (chassis no. 907-005), Sports/Prototype class, entered by Wicky Racing and driven by Wicky and Hanrioud. It retired in the 16th hour, after being in 21st place in the preceding hour. Wicky drove off the road when taken by surprise by a jammed accelerator.

Porsche no. 60. Type 910 (chassis no. 910-007), Sports/Prototype class, entered by Verrier and driven by Meier and Rouveyran. It retired in the 15th hour, after being in 25th place in the preceding hour. Trouble with a broken hub carrier, then brake problems, eliminated this Porsche.

Porsche no. 46. Type 910 (chassis no. 910-045), Sports/Prototype class, entered by Poirot and driven by Poirot and Krauss. It retired in the 14th hour, after being in 26th place in the preceding hour. Engine failure was the cause.

Porsche no. 20. Type 917 (chassis no. 917-043), entered by Wyer Automotive and driven by Siffert and Redman. It retired in the 12th hour, after being in fourth place in the preceding hour. Siffert was leading the field and going great guns when his engine over-revved and subsequently failed. He had had the third best time in practice: 3m 21.1s.

Porsche no. 18. Type 917 (chassis no. 910-021), entered by David Piper and driven by Piper and van Lennep. It retired in the 11th hour, after being in 20th place in the preceding hour.

The Finn Wihuri lent this 917 to David Piper to compete in the Le Mans 24 Hours. The car was between fifth and third places when Piper left the track. The car was badly damaged in this accident but was nevertheless repaired. Van Lennep took up the race, but then wrecked the bodywork on the Hunaudières straight.

Porsche no. 63. Type 911S, GTS class, entered by Rey Racing and driven by Rey and Chenevière. It retired in the 12th hour, after leaving the track. It had been in 19th place in the preceding hour.

Porsche no. 43. Type 911S, GTS class, entered by Gaban and driven by Gaban and Braillard. It retired in the tenth hour with a jammed gearbox, after being in 26th place in the preceding hour.

Porsche no. 59. Type 911S, GTS class, entered by Egreteaud and driven by Egreteaud and Mésange. It retired in the eighth hour with engine failure, after being in 31st place in the preceding hour.

Porsche no. 22. Type 917 (chassis no. 917-037), entered by Wyer Automotive and driven by Hailwood and Hobbs. It retired in the fifth hour, after being in 20th place in the preceding hour.

A second blow for the John Wyer team. Hailwood, who was driving the Porsche, was unable to avoid Facetti's Alfa Romeo which was in trouble on the Tertre Rouge S-bend. The resulting accident put this short-tail 917 out of the race.

Porsche no. 21. Type 917 (chassis no. 917-044), entered by Wyer Automotive and driven by Rodriguez and Kinnunen. None of the 917s entered by John Wyer finished the race. This one gave up in the fourth hour, after being in second place at the end of the first 60 minutes. The cooling fan broke, causing the Porsche to retire, by which time it had already dropped back to 48th place.

Race no.	Type Model	Engine position	Number of cylinders	Capacity in cc	Bore & stroke in mm	Valve operation	Cooling	Induction	Brakes	Transmission	Body material	Weight in kg (lb)
3	917	Rear	Flat-12	4494	85 x 66	4 ohc	air	injection	discs	Porsche 5+R	polyester	856 (1887)
18	917	Rear	Flat-12	4494	85 x 66	4 ohc	air	injection	discs	Porsche 4+R	polyester	826 (1821)
20	917	Rear	Flat-12	4907	86 x 70.4	4 ohc	air	injection	discs	Porsche 4+R	polyester	847 (1867)
21	917	Rear	Flat-12	4907	86 x 70.4	4 ohc	air	injection	discs	Porsche 4+R	polyester	845 (1863)
22	917	Rear	Flat-12	4494	85 x 66	4 ohc	air	injection	discs	Porsche 4+R	polyester	845 (1863)
23	917	Rear	Flat-12	4494	85 x 66	4 ohc	air	injection	discs	Porsche 4+R	polyester	810 (1786)
25	917	Rear	Flat-12	4907	86 x 70.4	4 ohc	air	injection	discs	Porsche 5+R	polyester	827 (1823)
27	908	Rear	Flat-8	2997	85 x 66	4 ohc	air	injection	discs	Porsche 5+R	polyester	648 (1429)
29	908/2	Rear	Flat-8	2997	85 x 66	4 ohc	air	injection	discs	Porsche 5+R	polyester	717 (1581)
40	914/6	Rear	Flat-6	1991	80 x 66	2 ohc	air	2 Weber	discs	Porsche 5+R	polyester	902 (1989)
42	911T	Rear	Flat-6	1991	80 x 66	2 ohc	air	2 Weber	discs	Porsche 5+R	steel	978 (2156)
43	911S	Rear	Flat-6	2195	84 x 66	2 ohc	air	2 Weber	discs	Porsche 5 +R	steel + polyester	902 (1989)
45	911S	Rear	Flat-6	2195	84 x 66	2 ohc	air	injection	discs	Porsche 5+R	steel	1058 (2332)
46	910	Rear	Flat-6	1991	80 x 66	2 ohc	air	injection	discs	Porsche 5+R	polyester	597 (1316)
47	911S	Rear	Flat-6	2253	85 x 66	2 ohc	air	2 Weber	discs	Porsche 5+R	steel	925 (2039)
59	911S	Rear	Flat-6	2247	85 x 66	2 ohc	air	2 Weber	discs	Porsche 5+R	steel + polyester	908 (2002)
60	910	Rear	Flat-6	1991	80 x 66	2 ohc	air	injection	discs	Porsche 5+R	polyester	599 (1321)
61	907	Rear	Flat-8	2195	80 x 54	4 ohc	air	injection	discs	Porsche 5+R	polyester	601 (1325)
62	911S	Rear	Flat-6	2195	84 x 66	2 ohc	air	2 Weber	discs	Porsche 5+R	steel	979 (2158)
63	911S	Rear	Flat-6	2247	85 x 66	2 ohc	air	2 Weber	discs	Porsche 5+R	steel + polyester	930 (2050)
64	911S	Rear	Flat-6	1991	80 x 66	2 ohc	air	2 Weber	discs	Porsche 5+R	steel	954 (2103)
65	911S	Rear	Flat-6	2247	85 x 66	2 ohc	air	2 Weber	discs	Porsche 5+R	steel + polyester	930 (2050)
66	911S	Rear	Flat-6	1991	80 x 66	2 ohc	air	2 Weber	discs	Porsche 5+R	steel	943 (2079)
67	911S	Rear	Flat-6	1991	80 x 66	2 ohc	air	2 Weber	discs	Porsche 5+R	steel	981 (2163)

1971

Thirty-three Porsches start, ten finish

The Porsche 917s ended their brief career in superb style at the 1971 Le Mans. Ended because the announcement of new rules for the World Championship would mean the exclusion of 5-litre 'monsters'. In superb style because for the second year running, a 917 came first in distance and in the Index of Performance. The 1971 event was remarkable for the smashing of the distance record at Le Mans (on whichever circuit) and for the attainment by certain of the 917s of 380km/h (236mph) on the Hunaudières straight! Finally, it was the record year for entries of Porsche cars – 33 Stuttgart machines were entered – and, above all, it was the last 'Le Mans start' in which the drivers had to dash across the track and leap in their vehicles. Truly, a page of motor racing history had been turned.

Porsche no. 22. Type 917 short-tail, entered by Martini Racing and driven by Marko and van Lennep. It was placed first in distance, covering 5335.31km (2315.21 miles) in 24 hours at an average 222.304km/h (138.13mph). It was also first in the Index of Performance and second in the Index of Efficiency.

With fifth best time in practice, this car could not have been more consistent. Starting modestly (eighth in the first hour), the Porsche made up ground as cars retired ahead of it and took, and held, the lead from the 13th hour, winning the triple crown: distance, Index of Performance and its class.

Porsche no. 19. Type 917 short-tail, entered by Wyer Automotive and driven by Müller and Attwood. It was second in distance, covering 5302.34km (3294.72 miles) in 24 hours at an average of 221.18km/h (137.43mph). It was also second in the Index of Performance and third in the Index of Efficiency.

The third Porsche from the Wyer stable, and the best: an intelligent race, free of serious problems, took it from seventh place in the first hour to second at the finish.

Porsche no. 63. Type 911S, GTS class, entered by A.S.A. Cachia-Bondy and driven by Touroul and 'Anselme'. It was placed sixth in distance, covering 4111.34km (2554.67 miles) in 24 hours at an average of 171.30km/h (106.44mph). It was also fourth in the Index of Performance and fifth in the Index of Efficiency. This was the best of the 911s, winning the GTS group and the 2.5-litre class.

Porsche no. 49. Type 907, Sports/Prototype class, entered by Wicky Racing and driven by Brun and Mattli. It came seventh in distance, covering 4110.96km (2554.43 miles) in 24 hours at an average of 171.29km/h (106.43mph). It was also 11th in the Index of Performance and 8th in the Index of Efficiency.

Engine trouble prevented this Swiss Porsche from doing better. It finished, nevertheless, but behind the first 911S driven by Touroul and 'Anselme'. However, it was placed first in the Sports/Prototype group.

Porsche no. 38. Type 911S, GTS class, entered by Mazzia and driven by Mazzia and Barth. It was eight in distance, covering 4077.36km (2533.55 miles) in 24 hours at an average of 169.89km/h (105.56mph). It also came fifth in the Index of Performance and fifth in the Index of Efficiency. Like the other 911s that crossed the finishing line, it was somewhat the worse for wear.

Porsche no. 42. Type 911S, GTS class, entered by Jean Mésange and driven by Mésange and 'Gedehem'. It was placed ninth in distance, covering 4007.73km (2490.29 miles) in 24 hours at an average of 166.98mph (103.76mph). It also came sixth in the Index of Performance and seventh in the Index of Efficiency.

Porsche no. 26. Type 911S, GTS class, entered by Koob and driven by Koob, Kremer and Huber. It came 10th in distance, covering 3924.71km (2438.70 miles) in 24 hours at an average of 163.52km/h (101.61mph). It was also sixth in the Index of Performance and thirteenth in the Index of Efficiency.

Porsche no. 39. Type 911S, GTS class, entered by the AGACI and driven by Verrier and Foucault. It was placed 11th in distance, covering 3901.85km (2424.50 miles) in 24 hours at an average of 162.57km/h (101.02mph). It also came eighth in the Index of Performance and ninth in the Index of Efficiency.

Porsche no. 44. Type 911S, GTS class, entered by Paul Watson Race Organization and driven by Vestey and Bond. It was placed 12th in the distance classification, covering 3849.58km (2392.01 miles) in 24 hours at an average of 160.40km/h (99.67mph). It was also 10th in the Index of Performance and 12th in the Index of Efficiency.

Porsche no. 36. Type 911S, GTS class, entered by Jean Sage and driven by Waldegård and Chenevière. It came 13th in distance, covering 3535.73km (2197.00 miles) in 24 hours at an average of 147.32km/h (91.54mph). It was also 13th in the Index of Performance and 9th in the Index of Efficiency.

Porsche no. 35. Type 911S, GTS class, entered by Greub, driven by Greub and Garant. It withdrew in the 20th hour, after being in 16th place in the preceding hour. This was the last Porsche to retire – with engine trouble – four hours from the finish.

Porsche no. 29. Type 908/2, Sports/Prototype class, entered by Wicky Racing and driven by Wicky and Cohen-Olivar. It retired in the 20th hour with gearbox trouble, after being in 10th place in the preceding hour.

Porsche no. 57. Type 917 short-tail, entered by Dominique Martin and driven by Martin and Pillon. It retired in the 20th hour, after being in 15th place in the preceding hour.

Not a very distinguished race – after the 18th best time in practice – for this 917 from the Zitro stable. It had a lot of trouble with its four-speed gearbox before retiring quite near to the finish.

Porsche no. 17. Type 917 long-tail, entered by Wyer Automotive and driven by Siffert and Bell. It retired in the 18th hour, after being in sixth place in the preceding hour.

A succession of troubles eliminated this last John Wyer long-tail. A transistor housing in the ignition system worked loose from the second hour and then a considerable leakage of oil occurred in the transmission casing: these faults forced the retirement.

Porsche no. 47. Type 911S, GTS class, entered by Wicky Racing and driven by Cochet and Selz. It retired in the 17th hour with a damaged universal joint, after being in 21st place in the preceding hour.

Porsche no. 30. Type 908/2, Sports/Prototype class, entered by Cosson and driven by Cosson and Leuze. It was disqualified for stopping for oil before completing the stipulated 25 laps; it had been in 12th place in the preceding hour.

Porsche no. 69. Type 914/6, GTS class, entered by Autohaus Max Moritz and driven by Quist and Krumm. It retired in the 15th hour with gearbox trouble, after being in 15th place in the preceding hour.

Porsche no. 28. Type 908/2, Sports/Prototype class, entered by Veuillet and driven by Ballot Lena and Chasseuil. It retired in the 14th hour, after being in 10th place in the preceding hour. This was the fastest of the Porsche 908s taking part, but unfortunately Chasseuil left the track at Maison Blanche on the Sunday morning, badly damaging the car, and was forced to retire.

Porsche no. 18. Type 917 long-tail, entered by Wyer Automotive and driven by Rodriguez and Oliver. It retired in the 14th hour, after being in sixth place in the preceding hour.

Rodriguez had the distinction of going to the front of the race at the end of the first hour, together with two other long-tail 917s. On the second time round he had already lapped Verrier's 911s bringing up the rear. Retirement, after this domination of the race, came in the middle of the night when an oil feed broke.

Porsche no. 65. Type 911s, GTS class, entered by Jacky Dechaumel, driven by Dechaumel and Parot. It was eliminated from the race in the 13th hour, after being in 31st place.

Porsche no. 23. Type 917/20 short-tail, entered by Martini Racing and driven by Jöst and Kauhsen. It retired in the 12th hour, after being in fifth place in the preceding hour.

This 917/20, nicknamed the 'Pink Pig', was an experimental car with a widened track foreshadowing the Porsche Can-Am Cars. Jöst went off the road at Arnage during the night. The car was severely damaged and there was no hope of restarting.

Porsche no. 41. Type 911S, GTS class, entered by Jean-Pierre Gaban, driven by Gaban and Braillard. It retired in the eighth hour with engine failure, after being in 33rd place in the preceding hour.

Porsche no. 40. Type 911S, GTS class, entered by Jean Egreteaud and driven by Egreteaud and Jacquemin. It retired in the eighth hour with a broken connecting rod, after being in 39th place in the preceding hour.

Porsche no. 33. Type 911S, GTS class, entered by Rey Racing and driven by Rey and Cassegrain. It retired in the 10th hour after its engine blew up; it had been in 35th place in the preceding hour.

Porsche no. 34. Type 911S, GTS class, entered by Richie Ginther Racing and driven by Johnson and Forbes-Robinson. It withdrew in the eighth hour with a broken connecting rod, after being in 36th place in the preceding hour.

Porsche no. 46. Type 914/6, GTS class, entered by Club Porsche Roman and driven by Sage and Keller. It retired in the ninth hour, after being in 28th place in the preceding hour. Of the two 914/6s that started neither finished: this one broke a connecting rod.

Porsche no. 37. Type 911S, GTS class, entered by Pierre Mauroy and driven by Lagniez and Mauroy. It retired in the seventh hour with gearbox trouble, after being in 34th place in the preceding hour.

Porsche no. 21. Type 917 long-tail, entered by Martini Racing and driven by Larrousse and Elford. It retired in the seventh hour, after being in 32nd place in the preceding hour.

This 917 had the second best time in practice and was close to the Rodriguez car on the starting line. Larrousse and Elford should have been able to achieve a good performance, but the bolts holding the cooling fan snapped, causing overheating and engine seizure.

Porsche no. 60. Type 908/2, Sports/Prototype class, entered by Claude Haldi and driven by Haldi and Weigel. It retired in the sixth hour with transmission problems, after being in 43rd place in the preceding hour.

Porsche no. 48. Type 911S, GTS class, entered by Jean-Pierre Hanrioud and driven by Hanrioud and Ilotte. It withdrew in the fourth hour with a cracked piston, after being in 44th place in the preceding hour.

Porsche no. 66. Type 911S, GTS class, entered by Rey Racing and driven by Geurie and Mathurin. It retired in the fourth hour with distributor problems, after being in 40th place in the preceding hour.

Porsche no. 43. Type 911S, GTS class, entered by Francois Migault and driven by Bodin and Courthiade. It retired in the third hour with a cracked piston, after being in 45th place in the preceding hour.

Porsche no. 27. Type 908/2, Sports/Prototype class, entered by Poirot and driven by Poirot and Andruet. It retired in the second hour after an accident with a Ferrari, when it had been in 47th place in the preceding hour.

Race no.	Type Model	Engine position	Number of cylinders	Capacity in cc	Bore & stroke in mm	Valve operation	Cooling	Induction	Brakes	Transmission	Body material	Weight in kg (lb)
17	917	Rear	Flat-12	4907	86 x 70.4	ohc	air	injection	discs	Porsche 5+R	polyester	927 (2044)
18	917	Rear	Flat-12	4907	86 x 70.4	ohc	air	injection	discs	Porsche 5+R	polyester	934 (2059)
19	917	Rear	Flat-12	4907	86 x 70.4	ohc	air	injection	discs	Porsche 5+R	polyester	940 (2072)
21	917	Rear	Flat-12	4907	86 x 70.4	ohc	air	injection	discs	Porsche 5+R	polyester	913 (2013)
22	917	Rear	Flat-12	4907	86 x 70.4	ohc	air	injection	discs	Porsche 5+R	polyester	885 (1951)
23	917	Rear	Flat-12	4907	86 x 70.4	ohc	air	injection	discs	Porsche 5+R	polyester	909 (2004)
26	911S	Rear	Flat-6	2380	87.5 x 66	ohc	air	2 Weber	discs	Porsche 5+R	steel + polyester	1057 (2330)

Race no.	Type Model	Engine position	Number of cylinders	Capacity in cc	Bore & stroke in mm	Valve operation	Cooling	Induction	Brakes	Transmission	Body material	Weight in kg (lb)
27	908/2	Rear	Flat-6	2380	87.5 x 66	ohc	air	2 Weber	discs	Porsche 5+R	polyester	666 (1468)
28	908/2	Rear	Flat-8	2997	85 x 66	ohc	air	injection	discs	Porsche 5+R	polyester	715 (1576)
29	908/2	Rear	Flat-8	2997	85 x 66	ohc	air	injection	discs	Porsche 5+R	polyester	724 (1596)
30	908/2	Rear	Flat-8	2997	85 x 66	ohc	air	injection	discs	Porsche 5+R	polyester	740 (1631)
33	911S	Rear	Flat-6	2380	87.5 x 66	ohc	air	2 Weber	discs	Porsche 5+R	steel + polyester	1042 (2297)
34	911S	Rear	Flat-6	2380	87.5 x 66	ohc	air	2 Weber	discs	Porsche 5+R	steel + polyester	1052 (2319)
35	911S	Rear	Flat-6	2380	87.5 x 66	ohc	air	injection	discs	Porsche 5+R	steel + polyester	1072 (2363)
36	911S	Rear	Flat-6	2380	87.5 x 66	ohc	air	injection	discs	Porsche 5+R	steel + polyester	1037 (2286)
37	911S	Rear	Flat-6	2380	87.5 x 66	ohc	air	2 Weber	discs	Porsche 5+R	steel + polyester	1060 (2237)
38	911S	Rear	Flat-6	2380	87.5 x 66	ohc	air	2 Weber	discs	Porsche 5+R	steel + polyester	977 (2154)
39	911S	Rear	Flat-6	2245	85 x 66	ohc	air	2 Weber	discs	Porsche 5+R	steel + polyester	982 (2165)
40	911S	Rear	Flat-6	2380	87.5 x 66	ohc	air	2 Weber	discs	Porsche 5+R	steel + polyester	946 (2086)
41	911S	Rear	Flat-6	2245	85 x 66	ohc	air	2 Weber	discs	Porsche 5+R	steel + polyester	969 (2136)
42	911S	Rear	Flat-6	2245	85 x 66	ohc	air	2 Weber	discs	Porsche 5+R	steel + polyester	972 (2143)
43	911S	Rear	Flat-6	1990	80 x 66	ohc	air	2 Weber	discs	Porsche 5+R	steel + polyester	936 (2064)
44	911S	Rear	Flat-6	2245	85 x 66	ohc	air	2 Weber	discs	Porsche 5+R	steel + polyester	992 (2187)
46	914/6	Rear	Flat-6	1990	80 x 66	ohc	air	2 Weber	discs	Porsche 5+R	steel + polyester	973 (2145)
47	911S	Rear	Flat-6	1990	80 x 66	ohc	air	2 Weber	discs	Porsche 5+R	steel + polyester	1036 (2284)
48	911S	Rear	Flat-6	2245	85 x 66	ohc	air	2 Weber	discs	Porsche 5+R	steel + polyester	1045 (2304)
49	907	Rear	Flat-8	1981	76 x 54	ohc	air	injection	discs	Porsche 5+R	polyester	687 (1515)
57	917	Rear	Flat-12	4494	85 x 66	ohc	air	injection	discs	Porsche 4+R	polyester	927 (2044)
60	908/2	Rear	Flat-8	2997	85 x 66	ohc	air	injection	discs	Porsche 5+R	polyester	729 (1607)
63	911S	Rear	Flat-6	2380	87.5 x 66	ohc	air	2 Weber	discs	Porsche 5+R	steel + polyester	1003 (2211)
65	911S	Rear	Flat-6	2245	85 x 66	ohc	air	2 Weber	discs	Porsche 5+R	steel + polyester	1061 (2339)
66	911S	Rear	Flat-6	2195	84 x 66	ohc	air	injection	discs	Porsche 5+R	steel + polyester	1028 (2266)
69	914/6	Rear	Flat-6	1991	80 x 66	ohc	air	2 Weber	discs	Porsche 5+R	steel + polyester	972 (2143)

1972

Fifteen Porsches start, four finish, of which one was not placed

The main features of the 1972 Le Mans were a new circuit of 13.64km (8.47 miles); the 'scratching' of the Ferraris at the last minute; and the Matra double. Official Porsches were conspicuously absent, the reason being that the doughty 917s, ineligible for the World Championship this year, were consigned to the museum. It was a dark year for the Stuttgart firm, represented only by old privately-entered cars; for France it was a renaissance as no French car had won at Le Mans since 1950 (the Rosier father and son in a Talbot). Henri Pescarolo and Graham Hill drove the winning Matra for 4691.34km (2915.06 miles) at an average 195.47km/h (121.46mph).

Porsche no. 60. Type 908 long-tail, entered by Siffert Team and driven by Jöst, Weber and Casoni. It was placed third in distance, covering 4428.90km (2751.99 miles) in 24 hours at an average of 184.53km/h (114.66mph). The three drivers of the Siffert Team took third place in a car that was showing its age, after a consistent race.

54

Porsche no. 41. Type 911S, GTS class, entered by Louis Meznarie and driven by Keyser, Barth and Garant. It came 13th in distance, covering 3883.67km (2413.30 miles) in 24 hours at an average of 161.81km/h (100.55mph).

With a sixth place in the Index of Efficiency this car had the best result of the seven 911s that started. It seemed very short-winded at the finish and not capable of going on much longer.

Porsche no. 24. Type 907, entered by Wicky Racing Team and driven by Mattli, Bayard and Brun. It was placed 18th in distance, covering 3431.61km (2132.30 miles) in 24 hours at an average 142.98km/h (88.84mph). Eighteenth and last, this was the third Porsche to be placed and its only merit was to finish.

Porsche no. 67. Type 908, entered by Christian Poirot and driven by Poirot and Farjon. This car finished but was not placed, not having covered the minimum distance required.

Porsche no. 5. Type 908/3, entered by the Escuderia Montjuich and driven by Fernandez, Torredemer and Baturone. It retired within a few laps of the finish after an accident, when it had been in eighth place.

Porsche no. 6. Type 908/2, entered by Weigel and Hans Dieter and driven by Krauss and Weigel. It retired in the 19th hour after it had left the track; it had been in ninth place in the preceding hour.

Porsche no. 65. Type 910, entered by Novestille and driven by Novestille and Ravenel. It retired in the 18th hour, because of a faulty bearing in a rear wheel, after being in 15th place in the preceding hour.

Porsche no. 42. Type 911S, GTS class, entered by Claude Haldi and driven by Haldi, Keller and 'Gedehem'. It retired in the 17th hour with engine trouble, after being in 19th place in the preceding hour.

Porsche no. 45. Type 911S, GTS class, entered by Raymond Touroul and driven by Bardini and Lee Banner. It retired in the 16th hour with engine trouble, after being in 28th place in the preceding hour.

Porsche no. 80. Type 911S, GTS class, entered by Porsche Kremer and driven by Fitzpatrick and Kremer. It retired in the fourth hour with a damaged crankshaft, after being in 41st place in the preceding hour.

Porsche no. 44. Type 911S, GTS class, entered by Jean Sage and driven by Sage, Loos and Pesch. It retired in the seventh hour with a damaged crankshaft, after being in 38th place in the preceding hour.

Porsche no. 79. Type 911S, GTS class, entered by Jean-Pierre Gaban and driven by Delbar and Vanderschriek. It retired in the third hour with a damaged driveshaft, after being in 37th place in the preceding hour.

Porsche no. 76. Type 908, entered by Jean Egreteaud and driven by Lagniez and Touroul. It retired in the seventh hour having run out of fuel; it had been in 31st place in the preceding hour.

Porsche no. 40. Type 911S, GTS class, entered by René Mazzia and driven by Mauroy and Mignot. It retired in the third hour with crankshaft damage, after being in 49th place in the preceding hour.

Porsche no. 58. Type 908/2, entered by Basch Racing and driven by Roser and Stuppacher. It retired after running off the track in the second hour; it had been in 42nd place in the preceding hour.

Race no.	Type Model	Engine position	Number of cylinders	Capacity in cc	Bore & stroke in mm	Valve operation	Cooling	Induction	Brakes	Transmission	Body material	Weight in kg (lb)
5	908/3	Rear	Flat-8	2997	85 x 66	ohc	air	injection	discs	Porsche 5+R	polyester	661 (1457)
6	908/2	Rear	Flat-8	2997	85 x 66	ohc	air	injection	discs	Porsche 5+R	polyester	659 (1453)
24	907	Rear	Flat-8	1981.5	76 x 54.6	ohc	air	injection	discs	Porsche 5+R	polyester	641 (1413)
40	911S	Rear	Flat-6	2498	86.8 x 70.2	ohc	air	injection	discs	Porsche 5+R	steel + polyester	970 (2138)
41	911S	Rear	Flat-6	2466	89 x 66	ohc	air	injection	discs	Porsche 5+R	steel + polyester	979 (2158)
42	911S	Rear	Flat-6	2492	86.7 x 70.4	ohc	air	injection	discs	Porsche 5+R	steel + polyester	984 (2169)
44	911S	Rear	Flat-6	2492	86.7 x 70.4	ohc	air	injection	discs	Porsche 5+R	steel + polyester	961 (2119)
45	911S	Rear	Flat-6	2492	86.7 x 70.4	ohc	air	2 Weber	discs	Porsche 5+R	steel + polyester	983 (2167)
58	908/2	Rear	Flat-8	2997	85 x 66	ohc	air	injection	discs	Porsche 5+R	polyester	689 (1519)
60	908	Rear	Flat-8	2997	85 x 66	ohc	air	injection	discs	Porsche 5+R	polyester	713 (1572)
65	910	Rear	Flat-6	2379	87.5 x 66	ohc	air	injection	discs	Porsche 5+R	polyester	587 (1294)
67	908	Rear	Flat-8	2997	85 x 66	ohc	air	injection	discs	Porsche 5+R	polyester	668 (1473)
76	908	Rear	Flat-8	2997	85 x 66	ohc	air	injection	discs	Porsche 5+R	polyester	673 (1484)
79	911S	Rear	Flat-6	2341	86.8 x 66	ohc	air	2 Weber	discs	Porsche 5+R	steel + polyester	982 (2165)
80	911S	Rear	Flat-6	2466	89 x 66	ohc	air	injection	discs	Porsche 5+R	steel + polyester	964 (2125)

Fifteen Porsches start, nine finish

This was a year of renaissance for Porsche. Its official entries – under the Martini colours – were the new Carrera RSRs, conceived for the Sports Racing category and fitted with 3-litre ohc engines developing some 315bhp. These new cars, easily recognizable by their aerodynamic devices, did not disappoint Stuttgart. The hope implicit in the RSRs was that they would compete out in front with the Matras and the Ferraris. In the end it was an all-French team that won. Pescarolo – again – and Larrousse covered 4853.94km (3016.10 miles) at an average speed of 202.24km/h (125.67mph) in their winning Matra.

Porsche no. 46. Type Carrera RSR, entered by Martini Racing and driven by Müller and van Lennep. It was placed fourth in the distance results, covering 4485.36km (2787.07 miles) in 24 hours at an average of 186.89km/h (116.12mph).

This was a good performance: the first Porsche place, behind two Matras and a Ferrari. It should be noted that the Carrera RSR had a 2998cc engine which had been achieved by boring out the 2.7-litre unit. This model was based on the 911S, but many detail modifications were made, particularly in the body-work: there were greatly widened wheelarches to take wheels of 11 inch width at the front and 14 inches at the rear. In practice this car lapped in 4m 14.9s.

Porsche no. 3. Type 908/3 (chassis no. 90803013), entered by Escuderia Montjuich and driven by Chenevière, Fernandez and Torredemer. It came fifth in distance, covering 4359.99km (2709.17 miles) in 24 hours at an average of 181.66km/h (112.88mph).

The three 908s all finished. No. 3 was the best prepared, and achieved the best placing. This 'Spanish' Porsche, prepared by Habeithur in Switzerland, experienced a few induction system troubles, but these did not prevent it from being placed.

Porsche no. 4. Type 908/2 (chassis no. 90802008), entered by Guillermo Ortega and driven by Ortega and Merello. It was placed seventh in distance, covering 4312.92km (2679.92 miles) at an average of 179.70km/h (111.66mph). A very creditable placing for this Ecuadorian team in a 1970 car that had already taken part in the previous year's Le Mans, with Weigel and Krauss at the wheel.

Porsche no. 45. Type Carrera (chassis no. 73/02), GTS class, entered by Porsche Kremer Racing and driven by Keller, Schickentanz and Kremer. It came eighth in distance, covering 4311.30km (2678.92 miles) at an average of 179.63km/h (111.64mph). There was also a victory in the Index of Efficiency for this Porsche, plus a second in the GT group, behind Elford's Ferrari Daytona.

Porsche no. 63. Type Carrera, entered by Gelo Racing and driven by Loos and Barth. It was in 10th place in distance, covering 4248.65km (2639.98 miles) in 24 hours at an average of 177.02km/h (109.99mph). It also came fifth in the Index of Efficiency.

Porsche no. 48. Type Carrera, GTS class, entered by Sonauto-BP Racing and driven by Gregg and Chasseuil. It took 14th place in distance, covering 4077.07km (2533.37 miles) in 24 hours at an average of 169.87km/h (105.55mph). It was also seventh in the Index of Efficiency.

This car experienced a number of problems: a puncture, cracked brake disc, damaged shock absorber, valve and accelerator linkage, etc. Although this was the best of the Porsches, the time it lost in the pits could not be made up.

Porsche no. 41. Type Carrera, GTS class, entered by Schiller Racing Team and driven by Selz and Vetsch. It was placed 16th in distance, covering 4061.86km (2523.92 miles) in 24 hours at an average of 169.24km/h (105.16mph). It also came sixth in the Index of Efficiency.

Porsche no. 42. Type Carrera, GTS class, entered by René Mazzia and driven by Mauroy and Mignot. It was 17th in the distance placings, covering 3965.26km (2463.90 miles) in 24 hours at an average of 165.21km/h (102.62mph). It was also ninth in the Index of Efficiency.

Porsche no. 52. Type 908/2 (chassis no. 90803009), entered by Wicky Racing and driven by Wicky, Cohen-Olivar and Carron. It was placed 21st in distance, covering 3688.72km (2292.06 miles) in 24 hours at an average of 153.69km/h (95.50mph). This 'old' car, dating from 1969, had a number of transmission problems which partly explains its modest performance.

Porsche no. 78. Type Carrera, GTS class, entered by Jean Sage and driven by Bayard and Ligonnet. It retired in the 10th hour with a cracked cylinder head, after being in 40th place in the preceding hour. The start of the race for this car was marked by dreadful roadholding and the tyres, prematurely worn out by excessive understeering, had to be changed. Then a broken piston brought retirement.

Porsche no. 49. Type Carrera, GTS class, entered by Jean Egreteaud and driven by Egreteaud and Lagniez. It retired in the 12th hour with transmission problems, after being in 33rd place in the preceding hour. This car had lost a lot of time after it ran off the road at Mulsanne, then more in changing the exhaust which had been damaged in the accident.

Porsche no. 43. Type Carrera, GTS class, entered by Max Moritz and driven by Quist, Zink and Laub. It withdrew in the ninth hour, after being in 35th place in the preceding hour. Before the end of the first hour, overheating problems were already worrying this team, whose car finally came to a standstill at Arnage.

Porsche no. 22. Type 910, entered by Raymond Touroul and driven by Touroul and Rouget. It retired in the 12th hour when it ran out of fuel, after being in 27th place in the preceding hour.

Porsche no. 44. Type Carrera, GTS class, entered by Club Porsche Roman and driven by Piot and Zbinden. It retired in the ninth hour after being in 28th place in the preceding hour. Piot had to stop in the first hour of the race with a displaced exhaust pipe. Then the gearbox gave up the ghost, forcing the team to withdraw.

Porsche no. 47. Type Carrera RSR, entered by Martini Racing and driven by Jöst and Haldi. It ran out of fuel in the sixth hour, after it had been in 42nd place in the preceding hour. An error in refuelling was the cause of this empty tank!

Race no.	Type Model	Engine position	Number of cylinders	Capacity in cc	Bore & stroke in mm	Valve operation	Cooling	Induction	Brakes	Transmission	Body material	Weight in kg (lb)
3	908/3	Rear	Flat-8	2997	85 x 66	ohc	air	injection	discs	Porsche 5+R	polyester	741 (1634)
4	908/2	Rear	Flat-8	2997	85 x 66	ohc	air	injection	discs	Porsche 5+R	polyester	657 (1448)
22	910	Rear	Flat-6	1991	80 x 66	ohc	air	injection	discs	Porsche 5+R	polyester	608 (1340)
41	Carrera	Rear	Flat-6	2807	90 x 70.4	ohc	air	injection	discs	Porsche 5+R	steel + polyester	951 (2097)
42	Carrera	Rear	Flat-6	2807	92 x 70.4	ohc	air	injection	discs	Porsche 5+R	steel + polyester	952 (2099)
43	Carrera	Rear	Flat-6	2807	92 x 70.4	ohc	air	injection	discs	Porsche 5+R	steel + polyester	952 (2099)
44	Carrera	Rear	Flat-6	2807	92 x 70.4	ohc	air	injection	discs	Porsche 5+R	steel + polyester	946 (2086)
45	Carrera	Rear	Flat-6	2807	92 x 70.4	ohc	air	injection	discs	Porsche 5+R	steel + polyester	960 (2116)
46	Carrera RSR	Rear	Flat-6	2998	95 x 70.4	ohc	air	injection	discs	Porsche 5+R	steel + polyester	883 (1947)
47	Carrera RSR	Rear	Flat-6	2998	95 x 70.4	ohc	air	injection	discs	Porsche 5+R	steel + polyester	883 (1947)
48	Carrera	Rear	Flat-6	2807	92 x 70.4	ohc	air	injection	discs	Porsche 5+R	steel + polyester	969 (2136)
49	Carrera	Rear	Flat-6	2807	92 x 70.4	ohc	air	injection	discs	Porsche 5+R	steel + polyester	913 (2013)
52	908/2	Rear	Flat-8	2997	85 x 66	ohc	air	injection	discs	Porsche 5+R	polyester	674 (1486)
63	Carrera	Rear	Flat-6	2807	92 x 70.4	ohc	air	injection	discs	Porsche 5+R	steel + polyester	952 (2099)
78	Carrera	Rear	Flat-6	2807	92 x 70.4	ohc	air	injection	discs	Porsche 5+R	steel + polyester	939 (2070)

1974

Twenty-two Porsches start, six finish

This was the third year in succession that Pescarolo and Matra won the 24-Hour Race at Le Mans. Once again Henri Pescarolo's partner in victory was Gerard Larrousse. They achieved 4606.57km (2862.39 miles) at an average speed of 191.94km/h (119/26mph). Porsche for its part came very close to victory, thanks to the Carrera RSR Turbo, which foreshadowed the 'Silhouette' category at Le Mans. These cars marked the promising advent of turbos for Porsche and for Le Mans. Note that the two RSR Turbos each developed some 450 to 510bhp, depending on tuning.

Porsche no. 22. Type Carrera RSR Turbo (chassis no. 010) Group 5, entered by Martini Racing and driven by van Lennep and Müller. It was placed second in distance, covering 4527.45km (2813.23 miles) in 24 hours at an average of 188.64km/h (117.21mph).

This was the fastest Porsche in practice. It started the race at the head of the second squad of cars, and far behind the leaders. It was towards 10am on Sunday morning that it began to have trouble with its steering, then with the gearbox. Without these incidents this Porsche would have staked a good claim to victory

Porsche no. 70. Type Carrera RSR, Group 4, entered by A.S.A. Cachia and Bondy and driven by Touroul, Rua and Cachia. It was 10th in distance, covering 3934.40km (2444.72 miles) in 24 hours at an average of 163.93km/h (101.83mph).

Touroul was the first victim of the failure of driveshaft joints on the Carreras and this slowed him down considerably. However, the race finished better that it started for this car. It would have done better still if a driveshaft had not had to be changed towards the end of the event.

Porsche no. 66. Type Carrera RSR, Group 4, entered by Porsche Club Roman and driven by Chenevière, Zbinden and Dubois. It came seventh in the distance results, covering 4260.95km (2647.63 miles) in 24 hours at an average of 177.53km/h (110.31mph).

Porsche no. 69. Type Carrera RSR (chassis no. 6840134), Group 4, entered by Lucien Nageotte and driven by Laffeach, Nageotte, Thiry and Jaunet. It came 12th in the distance placings, covering 3776.17km (2346.40 miles) in 24 hours at an average of 157.34km/h (99.76mph), after a consistent race slowed by over-long pit stops.

Porsche no. 59. Type Carrera RSR, Group 4, entered by Pierre Mauroy and driven by Verney, Mauroy and Renien. It came 13th in distance, covering 3773.33km (2344.63 miles) in 24 hours at an average of 157.22km/h (97.69mph). This car was held back by a number of troubles (radiator and shock absorber faults, fuel leakage, etc)

Porsche no. 63. Type Carrera RSR, Group 4, entered by Jean Claude Lagniez and driven by Lagniez, Méo and Egreteaud. It was placed 14th in distance, covering 3742.72km (2325.61 miles) in 24 hours at an average of 155.94km/h (96.90mph).

Méo had a slight collision, which damaged his car's rear lights, then Lagniez had some brake lines changed. These incidents cost a lot of time, explaining the mediocre performance.

Porsche no. 65. Type 908/2 (chassis no. 90802016), Group 5, entered by Christian Poirot and driven by Poirot and Rondeau. It was placed 19th for distance, covering 3433.66km (2133.57 miles) in 24 hours at an average of 143.06km/h (89.27mph).

This car failed to qualify for the 1973 Le Mans but a subsequent stay at the factory was worthwhile as it allowed the car to compete in 1974. However, trouble with the accelerator lost Rondeau three-quarters of an hour in repairs a long way from the pits. Later, problems with the exhaust, then a failing engine, slowed the car down and contributed to a less than brilliant finish.

Porsche no. 73. Type Carrera RSR, Group 4, entered by Paul Blancpain, driven by Keyser, Minter and Blancpain. It came 20th in the distance placings, covering 3367.37km (2092.38 miles) in 24 hours at an average of 140.30km/h (87.18mph). Changing the driveshaft joint, and a puncture, delayed this American Porsche considerably.

Porsche no. 72. Type Carrera RSR, (chassis no. 072) Group 4, entered by Polifac-Gelo Racing and driven by Pesch, Barth and Loos. It retired in the 22nd hour after being in 10th place in the preceding hour. A repair to the front left-hand mudguard and changing a shock absorber cost the team a lot of time. In the end a cracked piston compelled them to give up after a good recovery.

Porsche no. 62. Type Carrera RSR, Group 4, entered by Ecurie Francorchamps and driven by 'Beurlys', Bond and de Fierland. It retired in the 19th hour, after being in 10th place in the preceding hour.

'Beurlys' was back at Le Mans some ten years after his first exploits there. Clutch trouble caused the retirement of this Belgian Porsche.

Porsche no. 19. Type 908/2 (chassis no. 90803009), Group 5, entered by Wicky Racing and driven by Wicky, Boucard and Novestille. It retired in the sixth hour, after being in 37th place in the preceding hour.

Porsche no. 21. Type Carrera RSR Turbo (chassis no. 008), Group 5, entered by Martini Racing and driven by Koinigg and Schurti. It retired in the seventh hour, after being in 14th place in the preceding hour. A broken crankshaft forced this second Porsche Turbo to drop out at Mulsanne.

Porsche no. 64. Type Carrera RSR, Group 4, entered by Polifac/Gelo Racing and driven by Loos, Barth and Schickentanz. This car retired in the 13th hour of the race, having been in 25th place in the preceding hour.

The first stop for this car came in the first lap: a red warning light lit, but was a false alarm and the Porsche restarted. A little later, it had to retire because of gearbox trouble.

It was almost 2am when this Porsche came to a standstill after alternator problems.

Porsche no. 44. Type 910 (chassis no. 910-014) Group 5, entered by Gérard Guynet, driven by Guynet, Evrard and Gama. It retired, when it ran out of fuel, in the 17th hour, after being in 24th place in the preceding hour.

Porsche no. 67. Type Carrera RSR, Group 4, entered by Porsche Club Roman and driven by Chapuis, Vollery and Dorchy. It retired in the 19th hour, after being in 12th place in the preceding hour: the reason, a cracked piston.

Porsche no. 17. Type 908/2, Group 5, entered by the Ecuador-Marlboro Team and driven by Morello, Ortega and Ranft. It retired in the 10th hour, after being in 16th place in the preceding hour.

This was the fastest of the 8-cylinder cars. It was held up by a breakage in the fuel-injection pump drive. After this long delay the valiant Ecuadorian Porsche was doing well, recovering ground and moving up from 21st place to 7th place, when it ran off the road and out of the race.

Porsche no. 46. Type Carrera RSR, Group 5, entered by Rebaque Racing Team and driven by Rojas and Rebaque. It retired in the seventh hour, after being in 30th place in the preceding hour. This Mexican Porsche retired when its distributor drive broke – at a time when other retirements were helping it towards a good final placing.

Porsche no. 68. Type Carrera RSR, Group 4, entered by Samson Kremer Team, driven by Heyer, Kremer and Keller. It retired in the sixth hour, after being in 14th place in the preceding hour. Heyer achieved the best time in the GT category in practice. Unfortunately, his race was a short one; a cracked piston putting an end to his efforts.

Porsche no. 58. Type Carrera RSR, Group 4, entered by Escuderia Montjuich and driven by Haldi, Fernandez and Beguin. It retired in the sixth hour, after being in 35th place in the preceding hour.

After a good start, this car had to stop to change a silencer. However, the engine was affected and Beguin had hardly restarted when he had to stop again – and finally – with a broken valve spring.

Porsche no. 60. Type Carrera RSR, Group 4, entered by Louis Meznarie and driven by Striebig, Kirschoffer and Château. It retired in the fifth hour with a broken distributor drive, after being in 40th place in the preceding hour.

Porsche no. 61. Type Carrera RSR, Group 4, entered by Robert Buchet and driven by Vic Elford and Ballot Lena. It retired in the 11th hour, after being in 22nd place in the preceding hour.

This was the fastest of the RSRs, but after 19 hours Ballot Lena had to change a driveshaft, then in the middle of the night it was Elford's turn to carry out the same repair. Finally, at 1.45 in the morning, the transmission packed up.

Porsche no. 31. Type 908/3 (chassis no. 90803013) Group 5, entered by Escuderia Tibidabo and driven by Torredemer, Fernandez and Tramont. It retired in the fourth hour, after being in 42nd place in the preceding hour.

This car was placed fifth in 1973 with two of the same drivers. It had less of a chance this year, and had to retire after transmission and gearbox troubles.

Race no.	Type Model	Engine position	Number of cylinders	Capacity in cc	Bore & stroke in mm	Valve operation	Cooling	Induction	Brakes	Transmission	Body material	Weight in kg (lb)
17	908/2	Rear	Flat-8	2997	85 x 66	ohc	air	injection	discs	Porsche 5+R	polyester	668 (1473)
19	908/2	Rear	Flat-8	2997	85 x 66	ohc	air	injection	discs	Porsche 5+R	polyester	680 (1499)
21	Carrera RSR-T	Rear	Flat-6	2142 turbo	83 x 66	ohc	air	injection	discs	Porsche 5+R	steel + polyester	836 (1843)
22	Carrera RSR-T	Rear	Flat-6	2142 turbo	83 x 66	ohc	air	injection	discs	Porsche 5+R	steel + polyester	828 (1825)
31	908/3	Rear	Flat-8	2997	85 x 66	ohc	air	injection	discs	Porsche 5+R	polyester	694 (1530)
44	910	Rear	Flat-6 *m*	1998	82 x 66	ohc	air	injection	discs	Porsche 5+R	polyester	598 (1318)
46	Carrera RSR	Rear	Flat-6	2993	95 x 70.4	ohc	air	injection	discs	Porsche 5+R	steel + polyester	985 (2172)
58	Carrera RSR	Rear	Flat-6	2993	95 x 70.4	ohc	air	injection	discs	Porsche 5+R	steel + polyester	960 (2116)
59	Carrera RSR	Rear	Flat-6	2806	–	ohc	air	injection	discs	Porsche 5+R	steel + polyester	957 (2110)
60	Carrera RSR	Rear	Flat-6	2993	95 x 70.4	ohc	air	injection	discs	Porsche 5+R	steel + polyester	953 (2109)
61	Carrera RSR	Rear	Flat-6	2993	95 x 70.4	ohc	air	injection	discs	Porsche 5+R	steel + polyester	945 (2083)
62	Carrera RSR	Rear	Flat-6	2993	95 x 70.4	ohc	air	injection	discs	Porsche 5+R	steel + polyester	966 (2130)
63	Carrera RSR	Rear	Flat-6	2993	95 x 70.4	ohc	air	injection	discs	Porsche 5+R	steel + polyester	935 (2161)
64	Carrera RSR	Rear	Flat-6	2993	95 x 70.4	ohc	air	injection	discs	Porsche 5+R	steel + polyester	940 (2072)
65	908/2	Rear	Flat-8	2997	85 x 66	ohc	air	injection	discs	Porsche 5+R	polyester	640 (1411)
66	Carrera RSR	Rear	Flat-6	2993	95 x 70.4	ohc	air	injection	discs	Porsche 5+R	steel + polyester	963 (2123)
67	Carrera RSR	Rear	Flat-6	2993	95 x 70.4	ohc	air	injection	discs	Porsche 5+R	steel + polyester	980 (2161)
68	Carrera RSR	Rear	Flat-6	2993	95 x 70.4	ohc	air	injection	discs	Porsche 5+R	steel + polyester	995 (2194)
69	Carrera RSR	Rear	Flat-6	2993	95 x 70.4	ohc	air	injection	discs	Porsche 5+R	steel + polyester	980 (2161)
70	Carrera RSR	Rear	Flat-6	2993	95 x 70.4	ohc	air	injection	discs	Porsche 5+R	steel + polyester	940 (2072)
72	Carrera RSR	Rear	Flat-6	2993	95 x 70.4	ohc	air	injection	discs	Porsche 5+R	steel + polyester	955 (2105)
73	Carrera RSR	Rear	Flat-6	2993	95 x 70.4	ohc	air	injection	discs	Porsche 5+R	steel + polyester	983 (2167)

1975

Twenty-seven Porsches start, sixteen finish

A dull year for Le Mans, where a race of no great interest took place. The winners were Jacky Ickx and Derek Bell who in their Gulf covered 4595.57km (2855.55 miles) at an average of 191.48km/h (118.98mph). Porsche had no official entries because of the new fuel consumption rules. Notable among the large number of private Porsches was the first 930 Turbo to take part in the event, in the GT Experimental class. An interesting footnote is that in fact 28 Porsches started: an Equadorian Carrera, no. 29, which had not qualified, somehow slipped into the starting line-up and had done three laps before the organizers spotted the car and stopped it!

Porsche no. 15. Type 908/3 long-tail, Group 5, entered by Jöst Racing and driven by Jöst, Casoni and Barth. It came fourth in distance, covering 4440.51km (2759.20 miles) in 24 hours at an average of 185.02km/h (114.96mph).

The factory, officially absent from Le Mans, cooperated in preparing this long-tail 908. For a long time it was within striking distance of the leaders and had reached second place by dint of retirements when an accident cost it nearly an hour's delay. A great pity, for the car had been lapping with clockwork regularity.

Porsche no. 58. Type Carrera RSR, Group 4, entered by Gelo Racing Team and driven by Fitzpatrick and van Lennep. It came fifth in the distance placings, covering 4307.98km (2676.85 miles) in 24 hours at an average of 179.49km/h (111.53mph).

A fine victory in the GTS group for this team, which had been reinforced by Schurti in the trials. The consistency of this Porsche was exemplary, as was the pit work. It stopped for no more than 18 minutes altogether during the 24 hours. In this case the fastest car in the group was also the most durable, which is rare at Le Mans.

Porsche no. 69. Type Carrera RSR, Group 4, entered by Jean Blaton and driven by 'Beurlys', Faure and Cooper. It was placed sixth in distance, covering 4245.53km (2643.64 miles) in 24 hours at an average of 176.89km/h (109.91mph). This Belgian Porsche drove a consistent race without serious problems.

Porsche no. 53. Type Carrera RSR, Group 4, entered by A.S.A. Cachia and driven by Borras, Noisson and Cachia. It was seventh in distance, covering 4227.71km (2626.98 miles) in 24 hours at an average of 176.15km/h (109.45mph).

Porsche no. 84. Type Carrera RS, Group 3, entered by Gerhard Maurer, and driven by Maurer, Baez and Straehl. It came 10th in distance, covering 4037.11km (2508.54 miles) in 24 hours at an average of 168.21km/h (104.52mph). The three Swiss won their GT group, after lapping with a degree of regularity worthy of the country of clockmakers.

Porsche no. 55. Type Carrera RSR, Group 4, entered by Ecurie Robert Buchet and driven by Ballot Lena and Bienvenue. It came eighth in the distance placings, covering 4159.11km (2584.35 miles) in 24 hours at an average of 173.29km/h (107.68mph).

A succession of pit stops cost this Franco-Canadian team a lot of time: causes were a series of punctures, problems with an oil pipe and the cooling system.

Porsche no. 67. Type Carrera RS, Group 3, entered by Anny and Charlotte Verney and driven by Verney, Fontaine and Tarnaud. It came 11th in the distance placings, covering 4015.33km (2495.01 miles) in 24 hours at an average of 167.30km/h (103.95mph).

These three ladies could well have secured victory in the GT category (they consoled themselves with the Coupe des Dames) if their oil gauge had not become disconnected.

Porsche no. 65. Type Carrera RSR, Group 4, entered by Jägermeister Kremer and driven by 'Bill', Bellanos and Contreras. It was placed ninth in distance, covering 4156.60km (2582.54 miles) in 24 hours at an average of 173.19km/h (107.61mph).

Porsche no. 20. Type Carrera RSR, Group GTX, entered by Porsche Club Roman and driven by Beguin, Zbinden and Haldi. It was 15th in distance, covering 3966.22km (2464.49 miles) in 24 hours at an average of 165.26km/h (102.69mph).

There was a class victory for this, the only Porsche Turbo entered, despite trouble with the car's brakes and with its four-speed gearbox, which was a handicap on the bends.

Porsche no. 87. Type Carrera S, Group 3, entered by X-Racing and driven by Boubet and Dermagne. It took 20th place in distance covering 3839.95km (2386.03 miles) in 24 hours at an average of 159.99km/h (99.41mph). This car won the new 'Combined' index classification, consuming 25.5 litres/100km: a victory carried off despite brake trouble and leaving the road.

Porsche no. 77. Type Carrera RS, Group 3, entered by Phillippe Dagoreau and driven by Sabine, Dagoreau and Aeschlimann. It came 17th in the distance placings, covering 3875.88km (2408.36 miles) in 24 hours at an average of 161.49km/h (100.34mph). It was also third in Group 3, despite clutch trouble and a burst rear tyre.

Porsche no. 61. Type Carrera RSR, Group 4, entered by Ecurie Armagnac-Bigorre and driven by Bussi and Metral. It was placed 23rd in distance, covering 3616.29km (2247.06 miles) in 24 hours at an average of 150.679km/h (93.628mph). Changing the gearbox delayed this car, which nevertheless secured a placing.

Porsche no. 80. Type Carrera RS, Group 3, entered by X-racing and driven by Touroul and Hesnault. It was 18th in distance, covering 3869.26km (2404.25 miles) in 24 hours at an average of 162.21km/h (100.79mph). Touroul dominated his group after Wollek's troubles, but when a valve rocker broke, the car's engine was finished, bringing his efforts and hopes to nothing.

Porsche no. 63. Type Carrera RS, Group 3, entered by Porsche Club Roman and driven by Bering, Utz and Godel. It was placed 19th in distance, covering 3860.60km (2398.87 miles) in 24 hours at an average of 160.96km/h (100.02mph). A good effort unfortunately thwarted by a series of ignition problems.

Porsche no. 71. Type Carrera RSR, Group 4, entered by Joël Laplacette and driven by Pigeon, Leroux and Laplacette. It came 25th in the distance placings, covering 3512.56km (2182.60 miles) in 24 hours at an average of 146.35km/h (90.94mph). This team experienced serious problems with various fittings that worked loose, one after the other.

Porsche no. 50. Type Carrera RSR, Group 4, entered by Louis Meznarie, driven by Striebig, Kirschoffer and Mauroy. It was 28th in distance, covering 3301.38km (2051.38 miles) in 24 hours at an average of 137.55km/h (85.47mph).

A series of punctures, electrical problems and then trouble with the valve rockers and a piston necessitated an engine change and the loss of a great deal of time.

Porsche no. 78. Type Carrera RS, Group 3, entered by Ecurie Robert Suchet and driven by Wollek and Grandet. It retired from the race in the 24th hour, after being in 12th place in the preceding hour before making a premature pit stop for refuelling. Then Bob Wollek, leading the GT series group, went into a spin and damaged the car's exhaust, and was subsequently held up by a puncture.

Porsche no. 3. Type 908/2 (chassis no 9080216), Group 5, entered by Christian Poirot and driven by Poirot and Guynet. It retired in the 21st hour, after being in 10th place in the preceding hour. After a very consistent race, Christian Poirot's Porsche had to retire close to the finish with a damaged Cardan joint.

Porsche no. 1. Type 908/2, Group 5, entered by Wicky Racing and driven by Cohen-Olivar, Caron and Brachet. It retired in the 18th hour, after being in 35th place in the preceding hour. A series of clutch troubles slowed down and then eliminated this Porsche, which would never have been amongst the leaders anyway.

Porsche no. 59. Type Carrera RSR, Group 4, entered by Gelo Racing and driven by Schenken and Ganley. It retired in the 20th hour, after being in 35th place in the preceding hour. An engine and two gearbox changes seriously hampered this Porsche, and eventually caused its retirement close to the finish.

Porsche no. 57. Type Carrera RSR (chassis no. 002), Group 4, entered by Gante Racing and driven by Rulon, Miller, Waugh and Godard. It retired in the 10th hour, after being in 42nd place in the preceding hour. A faulty oil pipe ended this car's race.

Porsche no. 60. Type Carrera RSR, Group 4, entered by Gelo Racing and driven by Hezemans and Schurti. It retired from the race in the ninth hour, after being in 41st place in the preceding hour.

This car's drivers were backing up their team-mates Fitzpatrick and van Lennep, who took the GTS victory in another RSR; but were eliminated by a buckled wheel.

Porsche no. 68. Type Carrera RS, Group 4, entered by Guy Verrier and driven by Verrier, Vestey and Corthay. It retired in the ninth hour, after being in 36th place in the preceding hour. Guy Verrier had returned to Le Mans but without any luck — just a cracked cylinder head.

Porsche no. 83. Type Carrera RS, Group 3, entered by Jean-Yves Gadal and driven by Gadal and 'Segolen'. It retired in the fourth hour, after being in 52nd place in the preceding hour. A damaged distributor was the cause.

Porsche no. 52. Type Carrera RSR, Group 4, entered by Ecurie du Nord and driven by Vollery, Chapuis and Dorchy. It retired in the 11th hour, after being in 39th place in the preceding hour. It had a series of problems: a burst tyre and then a damaged engine valve.

Porsche no. 96. Type Carrera RS, Group 4, entered by Daniel Thiaw and driven by Nageotte and Picard. It retired in the sixth hour, after being in 26th place in the preceding hour.

No luck for this Porsche entered by a Senegalese which had to drop out with ignition trouble.

Porsche no. 16. Type Carrera RSR, Group 4, entered by Jöst Racing and driven by Schickentanz and Bertrams. It retired in the fourth hour, after being in 40th place in the preceding hour.

This Porsche's engine failed when the team demanded too much of it in chasing after Fitzpatrick: competition among the private entries had claimed its first victim ...

Race no.	Type Model	Engine position	Number of cylinders	Capacity in cc	Bore & stroke in mm	Valve operation	Cooling	Induction	Brakes	Transmission	Body material	Weight in kg (lb)
1	908/2	Rear	Flat-8	2977	85 x 66	ohc	air	injection	discs	Porsche 5+R	polyester	680 (1499)
3	908/2	Rear	Flat-8	2997	85 x 66	ohc	air	injection	discs	Porsche 5+R	polyester	633 (1395)
15	908/3	Rear	Flat-8	2997	85 x 66	ohc	air	injection	discs	Porsche 5+R	polyester	705 (1554)

Race no.	Type Model	Engine position	Number of cylinders	Capacity in cc	Bore & stroke in mm	Valve operation	Cooling	Induction	Brakes	Transmission	Body material	Weight in kg (lb)
16	Carrera RSR	Rear	Flat-6	2993	95 x 70.4	ohc	air	injection	discs	Porsche 5+R	steel + polyester	937 (2066)
20	Carrera RSR	Rear	Flat-6	2993 turbo	95 x 70.4	ohc	air	injection	discs	Porsche 4+R	steel + polyester	1148 (2531)
50	Carrera RSR	Rear	Flat-6	2993	95 x 70.4	ohc	air	injection	discs	Porsche 5+R	steel + polyester	–
52	Carrera RSR	Rear	Flat-6	2993	95 x 70.4	ohc	air	injection	discs	Porsche 5+R	steel + polyester	977 (2154)
53	Carrera RSR	Rear	Flat-6	2993	95 x 70.4	ohc	air	injection	discs	Porsche 5+R	steel + polyester	961 (2119)
55	Carrera RSR	Rear	Flat-6	2993	95 x 70.4	ohc	air	injection	discs	Porsche 5+R	steel + polyester	–
57	Carrera RSR	Rear	Flat-6	2993	95 x 70.4	ohc	air	injection	discs	Porsche 5+R	steel + polyester	1027 (2264)
58	Carrera RSR	Rear	Flat-6	2993	95 x 70.4	ohc	air	injection	discs	Porsche 5+R	steel + polyester	952 (2099)
59	Carrera RSR	Rear	Flat-6	2993	95 x 70.4	ohc	air	injection	discs	Porsche 5+R	steel + polyester	946 (2086)
60	Carrera RSR	Rear	Flat-6	2993	95 x 70.4	ohc	air	injection	discs	Porsche 5+R	steel + polyester	950 (2094)
61	Carrera RSR	Rear	Flat-6	2993	95 x 70.4	ohc	air	injection	discs	Porsche 5+R	steel + polyester	942 (2077)
63	Carrera RS	Rear	Flat-6	2993	95 x 70.4	ohc	air	injection	discs	Porsche 5+R	steel + polyester	1012 (2231)
65	Carrera RSR	Rear	Flat-6	2993	95 x 70.4	ohc	air	injection	discs	Porsche 5+R	steel + polyester	947 (2088)
67	Carrera RS	Rear	Flat-6	2993	95 x 70.4	ohc	air	injection	discs	Porsche 5+R	steel + polyester	1016 (2240)
68	Carrera RS	Rear	Flat-6	2993	95 x 70.4	ohc	air	injection	discs	Porsche 5+R	steel + polyester	970 (2138)
69	Carrera RSR	Rear	Flat-6	2993	95 x 70.4	ohc	air	injection	discs	Porsche 5+R	steel + polyester	956 (2108)
71	Carrera RSR	Rear	Flat-6	2993	95 x 70.4	ohc	air	injection	discs	Porsche 5+R	steel + polyester	940 (2072)
77	Carrera RS	Rear	Flat-6	2993	95 x 70.4	ohc	air	injection	discs	Porsche 5+R	steel + polyester	984 (2169)
78	Carrera RS	Rear	Flat-6	2993	95 x 70.4	ohc	air	injection	discs	Porsche 5+R	steel + polyester	1202 (2650)
80	Carrera RS	Rear	Flat-6	2993	95 x 70.4	ohc	air	injection	discs	Porsche 5+R	steel + polyester	940 (2072)
83	Carrera RS	Rear	Flat-6	2687	90 x 70.4	ohc	air	injection	discs	Porsche 5+R	steel + polyester	988 (2178)
84	Carrera RS	Rear	Flat-6	2993	95 x 70.4	ohc	air	injection	discs	Porsche 5+R	steel + polyester	1005 (2216)
87	Carrera S	Rear	Flat-6	2687	90 x 70.4	ohc	air	injection	discs	Porsche 5+R	steel + polyester	974 (2147)
96	Carrera RS	Rear	Flat-6	2993	95 x 70.4	ohc	air	injection	discs	Porsche 5+R	steel + polyester	942 (2077)

1976

Twenty-six Porsches start, fourteen finish and two are unplaced

An historic Le Mans victory for a turbocharged car. Twenty-five years after its debut in the event, Porsche triumphed again, its 936 Turbo asserting its domination of the distance classification and of Group 6. Also the 935 dominated Group 5, as did the Carrera Group 4. Another Carrera won the American IMSA category. A quarter of a century after Veuillet and Mouche achieved a class win in the first Porsche participation at Le Mans, this third overall victory fully justified the efforts made at Zuffenhausen to secure domination of an event of this order. In addition, to demonstrate its commitment to the Le Mans 24 hours, Porsche had returned there, to win, with a new two-seater sports model, the 936.

Porsche no. 20. Type 936 (chassis no. 936 002) Group 6, entered by Martini Racing and driven by Ickx and van Lennep. It came first in distance, covering 4769.92km (2963.89 miles) in 24 hours at an average of 198.74km/h (123.49mph).

The third Le Mans victory for Jacky Ickx, and the second for van Lennep — and not due to chance. Once the Renault Alpine had disappeared only the Gulf could contest the Porsche's supremacy — in vain!

Porsche no. 40. Type 935, Group 5, entered by Martini Racing and driven by Stommelen and Schurti. It was placed fourth on distance, covering 4521.29km (2809.40 miles) in 24 hours at an average of 186.38km/h (115.81mph).

Despite its tremendous thirst (60 litres to the 100km), this Porsche 935 remained among the front runners until serious trouble occurred in the form of a puncture which badly damaged the rear left-hand side of the car. Then it was slowed down by ignition problems and the replacement of a turbocharger: nevertheless it succeeded in finishing in a more than creditable fourth place.

Porsche no. 52. Type Carrera, Group 5, entered by Gérard Méo and driven by Touroul and Cudini. It was placed sixth on distance, covering 4388.83km (2727.09 miles) in 24 hours at an average of 178.70km/h (111.04mph). This car won the category with a comfortable 13-lap lead over the following car in the class.

Porsche no. 17. Type 908/3, Group 6, entered by Jöst Racing Team and driven by Krauss and Steckonig. It came seventh on distance, covering 4276.87km (2657.34 miles) in 24 hours at an average of 178.20km/h (110.73mph).

Porsche no. 63. Type Carrera, Group 5, entered by Egon Evertz KG and driven by Bertrams, Martin and Evertz. It was placed ninth in distance covering 4131.74km (2567.52 miles) in 24 hours at an average of 172.15km (106.97mph).

This car also finished second in Group 5, 13 laps behind Touroul's Porsche no. 52.

Porsche no. 54. Type 934, Group 5, entered by Louis Meznarie and driven by Striebig, Verney and Kirschoffer. It came 11th in distance, covering 4068.50km (2528.04 miles) in 24 hours at an average of 169.52km/h (105.33mph).

A good début for this team, which included a woman as capable as the best male drivers. Unfortunately, the car was slowed by repeated oil leaks.

Porsche no. 53. Type Carrera, Group 5, entered by A.S.A Cachia-Bondy and driven by Sabine, Dagoreau, Andruet and Cachia. It was placed 13th in distance, covering 3930.14km (2442.08 miles) in 24 hours at an average of 163.75km/h (101.75mph).

Despite a nasty shock when the fuel-injection cut out on the track, the driver succeeded in regaining the pits where the mechanics were able to repair it.

Porsche no. 57. Type 934, Group 4, entered by Gelo Racing Team and driven by Hezemans and Schenken. It was 16th in the distance classification, covering 3791.73km (2356.07 miles) in 24 hours at an average of 157.93km/h (98.13mph).

This car was dominating Group 4 (GT) when a transmission problem forced it to return to the pits at reduced speed. It took 2 hours and 30 minutes to put matters right: the car finished second in its group.

Porsche no. 77. Type Carrera, IMSA Group, entered by Tom Waugh and driven by Rulon, Waugh and Laffeach. It came 14th in distance, covering 3866.51km (2402.54 miles) in 24 hours at an average of 161.10km/h (100.10mph).

The American cars contesting this category retired and this Porsche continued to lap with great regularity, so it was logical that it should reap the rewards of its consistent performance. It won the IMSA category, in which it was the sole surviver.

Porsche no. 67. Type Carrera, Group 4, entered by Joël Laplacette, driven by Laplacette, Leroux, and Bourdillat. It was placed 17th in distance, covering 3736.56km (2321.79 miles) in 24 hours at an average of 155.69km/h (96/74mph).

This car had problems with its electrics, a Cardan joint, and than left the road on Sunday morning — but this did not prevent it finishing third in its group!

Porsche no. 50. Type Carrera, Group 5, entered by Thierry Perrier and driven by Perrier, Renier and de Saint-Pierre. It came 18th in the distance placings, covering 3726.26km (2315.39 miles) in 24 hours at an average of 155.26km/h (96.47mph). Electrical problems held this car back.

Porsche no. 71. Type Carrera, Group 4, entered by 'Segolen' and driven by 'Segolen', Ouvière and Gadal. It came 12th on distance, covering 3987.93km (2477.98 miles) in 24 hours at an average of 166.16km/h (103.24mph).

The Bretons, after a very consistent performance and the retirement of Schenken and then Chenevière, found themselves in the lead in their group. They had a very creditable victory in the GT group in which 10 Porsches had been entered.

Porsche no. 65. Type 934, Group 4, entered by Kremer Racing and driven by Beaumont, Wollek and Pironi. It came 19th in distance, covering 3683.95km (2289.10 miles) at a average of 153.49km/h (95.37mph).

It was certainly a good team in this car, but the drivers were unable to give of their best because of the car's faulty clutch (it was changed twice).

Porsche no. 55. Type Carrera, Group 5, entered by Ecurie Almeras and driven by Boubet and Poirot. It was 23rd in the distance placings, covering 3355.10km (2084.76 miles) in 24 hours at an average of 139.79km/h (86.86mph).

After repeated electrical short circuits, the mechanics changed the entire electric system (which would take a week at your nearest Porsche agent!). All this work just to finish — but a splendid gesture!

Porsche no. 61. Type 934, entered by A.S.A. Cachia-Bondy and driven by Andruet, Borras and Cachia. It was not placed, having covered an insufficient distance. Although it started very fast, a change of turbocharger, defective valves, a second turbocharger replacement, and finally a large oil leak delayed this car considerably.

Porsche no. 70. Type 934, entered by 'Beurlys' and driven by 'Beurlys', Faure and Goss. It was not placed, not having covered the stipulated minimum distance.

A first stop 30 minutes after the start (with a burst tyre) cost some time — but this was only the start of the car's troubles. The heat exchanger, and above all the replacement of a tubocharge on four occasions, considerably slowed down this Belgian Porsche.

Porsche no. 47. Type 935, Group 5, entered by Kremer Racing and driven by Heyer, Bolanos, Negrete and Sprowls. It withdrew in the 24th hour, after being timed in 19th place in the preceding hour.

At midnight the clutch had to be changed, necessitating partial dismantling of the engine. On Sunday morning there were problems with turbo cooling then, the cause of the retirement, there was a fire. This was soon under control, but did a lot of damage.

Porsche no. 58. Type 934, entered by Porsche Club Roman and driven by Chenevière, Zbinden and Buehrer. It retired in the 23rd hour, after being in 12th place in the preceding hour. For a time this Porsche led its group, but fate and engine failure decided that this was not to continue

Porsche no. 69. Type 934, Group 4, entered by Schiller Racing Team and driven by Haldi and Vetsch. It retired in the 19th hour, after being in 14th place in the preceding hour. Engine failure caused the retirement when the car was lying second behind the Group 4 leader.

Porsche no. 18. Type 936, Group 6 (chassis no. 936001), entered by Jöst Racing Team and driven by Jöst and Barth. It retired in the 16th hour, after being in sixth place in the preceding hour.

A damaged engine put a stop to the superb race run by this car, which held second place for some 15 hours (except during change-overs).

Porsche no. 78. Type Carrera, IMSA Group, entered by Diego Febles Racing and driven by Febles, Poole and Cruz. It retired in the 15th hour, after being in 29th place in the preceding hour. Towards six o'clock in the morning this Porsche's gearbox began to show signs of fatigue, forcing a retirement a few minutes later.

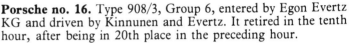

Porsche no. 16. Type 908/3, Group 6, entered by Egon Evertz KG and driven by Kinnunen and Evertz. It retired in the tenth hour, after being in 20th place in the preceding hour.

Porsche no. 72. Type Carrera, Group GTX, entered by Vollery and driven by Aeschlimann, Vollery and Dorchy. It retired in the ninth hour, after being in 37th place in the preceding hour.

This car should have won the GTX Group, in which it was the only entrant left in the race. Electrical trouble out on the circuit, far from the pits, forced its retirement.

Porsche no. 49. Type Carrera, Group 5, entered by Gelo Racing Team and driven by Schickentanz and Ganley. It retired in the sixth hour, after being in 22nd place in the preceding hour.

Porsche no. 62. Type Carrera, Group 4, entered by Philippe Dagoreau and driven by Gurdjian, Bussi, and Gouttepifre. It retired in the eight hour, after being in 39th place in the preceding hour.

A damaged engine caused its retirement after minor troubles with the accelerator and sparkplugs.

Porsche no. 48. Type 934, Group 5, entered by Jean-Louis Château and driven by Château, Geurie and Fornage. It retired in the sixth hour, after being in 48th place in the preceding hour.

Gearbox faults, that could not be repaired, developed less than three hours after the start and put an end to this car's race.

Race no.	Type Model	Engine position	Number of cylinders	Capacity in cc	Bore & stroke in mm	Valve operation	Cooling	Induction	Brakes	Transmission	Body material	Weight in kg (lb)
16	908/3	Rear	Flat-6	2142	83 x 66	ohc	air	injection	discs	Porsche 5+R	polyester	700 (1543)
17	908/3	Rear	Flat-6	2142 turbo	83 x 66	ohc	air	injection	discs	Porsche 5+R	polyester	700 (1543)
18	936	Rear	Flat-6	2142 turbo	83 x 66	ohc	air	injection	discs	Porsche 5+R	polyester	700 (1543)
20	936	Rear	Flat-6	2142 turbo	83 x 66	ohc	air	injection	discs	Porsche 5+R	polyester	700 (1543)
40	935	Rear	Flat-6	2847 turbo	92 x 70.4	ohc	air	injection	discs	Porsche 4+R	steel + polyester	970 (2138)
47	935	Rear	Flat-6	2847 turbo	92 x 70.4	ohc	air	injection	discs	Porsche 5+R	steel + polyester	970 (2138)
48	934	Rear	Flat-6	2993 turbo	95 x 70.4	ohc	air	injection	discs	Porsche 5+R	steel + polyester	–
49	Carrera	Rear	Flat-6	2993	95 x 70.4	ohc	air	injection	discs	Porsche 5+R	steel + polyester	–
50	Carrera	Rear	Flat-6	2993	95 x 70.4	ohc	air	injection	discs	Porsche 5+R	steel + polyester	860 (1896)
52	Carrera	Rear	Flat-6	2993	95 x 70.4	ohc	air	injection	discs	Porsche 5+R	steel + polyester	945 (2083)
53	Carrera	Rear	Flat-6	2993	95 x 70.4	ohc	air	injection	discs	Porsche 5+R	steel + polyester	–
54	934	Rear	Flat-6	2993 turbo	95 x 70.4	ohc	air	injection	discs	Porsche 5+R	steel + polyester	1120 (2469)
55	Carerra	Rear	Flat-6	2993	95 x 70.4	ohc	air	injection	discs	Porsche 5+R	steel + polyester	1150 (2535)
57	934	Rear	Flat-6	2993 turbo	95 x 70.4	ohc	air	injection	discs	Porsche 5+R	steel + polyester	–
58	934	Rear	Flat-6	2993 turbo	95 x 70.4	ohc	air	injection	discs	Porsche 5+R	steel + polyester	1120 (2469)
61	934	Rear	Flat-6	2993 turbo	95 x 70.4	ohc	air	injection	discs	Porsche 5+R	steel + polyester	–
62	Carrera	Rear	Flat-6	2993	95 x 70.4	ohc	air	injection	discs	Porsche 5+R	steel + polyester	900 (1984)
63	Carrera	Rear	Flat-6	2993	95 x 70.4	ohc	air	injection	discs	Porsche 5+R	steel + polyester	1120 (2469)
65	934	Rear	Flat-6	2993 turbo	95 x 70.4	ohc	air	injection	discs	Porsche 5+R	steel + polyester	1120 (2469)
67	Carrera	Rear	Flat-6	2993	95 x 70.4	ohc	air	injection	discs	Porsche 5+R	steel + polyester	940 (2072)
69	934	Rear	Flat-6	2993 turbo	95 x 70.4	ohc	air	injection	discs	Porsche 5+R	steel + polyester	1120 (2469)
70	934	Rear	Flat-6	2993 turbo	95 x 70.4	ohc	air	injection	discs	Porsche 5+R	steel + polyester	1120 (2469)
71	Carrera	Rear	Flat-6	2993	95 x 70.4	ohc	air	injection	discs	Porsche 5+R	Steel + polyester	1100 (2425)
72	Carrera	Rear	Flat-6	2993	95 x 70.4	ohc	air	injection	discs	Porsche 5+R	steel + polyester	1100 (2425)
77	Carrera	Rear	Flat-6	2993	95 x 70.4	ohc	air	injection	discs	Porsche 5+R	steel + polyester	945 (2083)
78	Carrera	Rear	Flat-6	2993	95 x 70.4	ohc	air	injection	discs	Porsche 5+R	steel + polyester	945 (2083)

1977

Twenty-five Porsches start, nine finish

This year's Le Mans was a race that saw new developments and the first serious tussle between the Porsche and Renault turbos. For the first time in the history of Le Mans there were three men on the winner's podium to shake the victory champagne: Jacky Ickx (for the fourth time), Jürgen Barth and Hurley Haywood. The latter two, whom Ickx came to help after his own car went out of the race, staged a remarkable recovery that did not let up until the finish.

Porsche no. 4. Type 936 (chassis no. 936001), Group 6, entered by Martini Racing and driven by Barth, Haywood and Ickx. It was placed first in distance, covering 4671.63km (2902.81 miles) in 24 hours at an average of 194.65km/h (120.95mph).

Four hours after the start there was an alarm concerning the fuel-injection pump. Jacky Ickx had retired his own car by this time, so came to lend the Barth-Haywood team a hand. Starting from 41st place, their progress from 8.00pm on Saturday continued inexorably, until the end of the race was in sight and the Porsche lost the use of a piston. Barth then had the difficult task of nursing the car to the finish, which he did, crossing the line as winner but leaving behind a worrying trail of blue smoke.

Porsche no. 40. Type 935, Group 5, entered by JMS Racing Team and driven by Ballot Lena and Gregg. It was third in the distance placings, covering 4307.53km (2676.57 miles) in 24 hours, at an average of 179.48km/h (111.52mph).

After a lot of trouble — a change of turbocharger, problems with brakes and the fuel-injection pump — this Franco-American team performed miracles, securing for themselves not only a third in distance but victory in Group 5.

Porsche no. 58. Type 934, Group 4, entered by Kremer Racing and driven by Wollek, Steve and Gurdjian. It was seventh in distance, covering 4066.07km (2526.53 miles) in 24 hours at an average of 169.41km/h (105.27mph).

After a brilliant start, troubles developed that slowed the progress of this Porsche: a Cardan joint, steering and then the suspension all developed problems. Fortunately its competitors in the group were not spared mechanical problems either, so this car regained the lead and won its group.

Porsche no. 61. Type Carrera, Group 4, entered by Gouttepifre and driven by Gouttepifre, Malbran and Leroux. It was placed 10th in distance, covering 3844.08km (2388.60 miles) in 24 hours at an average of 160.17km/h (99.52mph). A good placing

for this Porsche, which had no trouble except with its rear-view mirrors!

Porsche no. 70. Type Carrera, IMSA Group, entered by A.S.A. Cachia and driven by Latour, Delaunay and Guerin. It was placed 12th in distance, covering 3762. 90km (2338.15 miles) in 24 hours at an average of 156.78km/h (97.42mph).

It was beaten by two BMWs in the IMSA category, taking third place, but a long way behind the winners.

Porsche no. 79. Type Carrera, IMSA Group, entered by Jean-Louis Ravenel and driven by Ravenel, Ravenel and Detrin. It came 14th in distance, covering 3755.64km (2333.64 miles) in 24 hours at an average of 156.48km/h (97.35mph). It finished fourth in its group.

Porsche no. 47. Type Carrera, Group 5, entered by A.C. Verney and driven by Verney, Metge and Snobeck. It came 18th in the distance placings covering 3467.89km (2154.84 miles) in 24 hours at an average of 144.49km/h (89.78mph).

After having changed a Cardan joint, the mechanics had to take out the engine in order to change the gearbox. All of this caused a delay, but did not prevent the team taking second place in Group 5.

Porsche no. 56. Type 934, Group 4, entered by JMS Racing Team and driven by Bousquet, Dagoreau and Grandet. It was 19th in the distance rankings, covering 3451.86km (2144.88 miles) in 24 hours at an average of 143.82km/h (89.37mph).

Leaving the track twice made work for the mechanics, who also had to change a turbocharger on the Sunday morning. This delayed the 934 considerably, but it nevertheless finished third in Group 4.

Porsche no. 77. Type Carrera, IMSA Group, entered by Wynn's International and driven by Kirby, Hotchkiss and Aase. It was placed 20th in distance, covering 3367.34km (2092.36 miles) in 24 hours at an average of 140.30km/h (87.18mph). This was well and truly the last of the placed Porsches — but at least it did finish after a lot of difficulties.

Porsche no. 39. Type 935, Group 5, entered by Gelo Racing Team and driven by Hezemans, Schenken, Hayer and Ludwig. It retired in the 22nd hour, after being in seventh place in the preceding hour.

This car was well on its way to a remarkable group victory when its engine decided otherwise. Earlier, this Porsche had been rubbing shoulders with the best of Group 6, and for some hours it had even been in third place overall.

Porsche no. 80. Type Carrera, IMSA Group, entered by Bernard Beguin and driven by Beguin, Boubet and Briavoine. It withdrew in the 18th hour with cylinder head problems after being in 19th place in the preceding hour.

Porsche no. 96. Type Carrera, Group GTX, entered by GVEA and driven by Savary, Corthay and Salamin. It retired in the 20th hour, after being in 18th place in the preceding hour.

The only Porsche entered in the GTX group, it had to retire quite close to the finish with cylinder head problems.

Porsche no. 57. Type 934, Group 4, entered by Koob and driven by Braillard, Koob and Ortega. It retired in the 15th hour with turbocharger trouble after being in 31st place in the preceding hour.

Porsche no. 78. Type Carrera, IMSA Group, entered by Charles Ivey Engineering and driven by Rulon, Cooper and Waugh. It retired in the 18th hour with a damaged distributor after being in 21st place in the preceding hour.

Porsche no. 63. Type Carrera, Group 4, entered by Lapacette and driven by Laplacette, Courage and 'Segolen'. It retired in the 14th hour with Cardan joint damage after being in 33rd place in the preceding hour.

Porsche no. 59. Type 934, Group 4, entered by Heinz Schiller and driven by Servanin, Hummel and Ferrier. It retired in the 14th hour, after being in 11th place in the preceding hour. Despite a brilliant performance in the first 12 hours, this car, like no. 60, did not cover half the minimum distance.

Porsche no. 60. Type 934, Group 4, entered by Heinz Schiller and driven by Haldi, Vetsch and Pallavicini. It retired in the 11th hour after being logged in 17th place in the preceding hour. For a long time this car was the best in its group, but unfortunately it did not pass the halfway mark.

Porsche no. 48. Type Carrera, Group 5, entered by Thierry Perrier and driven by Perrier, Belliard and Leroux. It retired in the 11th hour, after being in 39th place in the preceding hour: the cause was a damaged gearbox.

Porsche no. 55. Type 934, Group 4, driven by Fernandez, Baturone and Tarredas. It retired in the 10th hour, with piston ring trouble, after being in 26th place in the preceding hour.

Porsche no. 49. Type Carrera, Group 5, entered by Hubert Striebig and driven by Chasseuil, Striebig and Kirschoffer. It retired in the sixth hour, after being in 24th place in the preceding hour. A damaged cylinder head gasket caused the retirement of this 'false silhouette' Carrera.

Porsche no. 62. Type Carrera, Group 4, entered by Bourdillat and driven by Bourdillat, Sotty and Bernard. It retired in the sixth hour with a damaged engine after being in 39th place in the preceding hour.

Porsche no. 41. Type 935, Group 5, entered by Martini Racing and driven by Stommelen and Schurti. It retired in the fourth hour, after being in 18th place in the preceding hour.

Jabouille, in his Renault, set off very quickly and it was Stommelen who tried to go after him. This endeavour did not allow for a small oil leak, the repair of which lost him about 40 places when he stopped to refuel. Stommelen and Schurti were attempting to make up for this when the car's engine packed up. Note that this 935 was fitted with a double turbocharger, like the two 936s.

Porsche no. 3. Type 936 (chassis no. 936002), Group 6, entered by Martini Racing and driven by Ickx and Pescarolo. It retired in the fourth hour, after being in fourth place in the preceding hour.

Despite holding back a little, the star team of the 1977 Le Mans were soon aware of the weakness of their car's engine. A connecting rod worked loose at about 6.50pm, causing retirement. It was an anxious time for the Porsche camp, who saw three Renaults and a Mirage in the lead. However, the race was not over, not for Porsche nor for Jacky Ickx, who transferred to the 936 no. 4. Note that the two 936s were fitted with double turbochargers for the first time.

Porsche no. 38. Type 935, Group 5, entered by Gelo Racing Team and driven by Schenken, Hezemans and Heyer. It retired in the second hour, after being in 54th place in the preceding hour.

As this car went so early its drivers transferred to the no. 39 Porsche from the same stable, in which they performed brilliantly until their car's engine failed close to the finish.

Porsche no. 42. Type 935, Group 5, entered by Kremer Racing and driven by Fitzpatrick, Edwards and Faure. It retired in the second hour, after being in 16th place in the preceding hour. The car was on the 14th lap when its engine blew up, forcing the retirement.

Race no.	Type Model	Engine position	Number of cylinders	Capacity in cc	Bore & stroke in mm	Valve operation	Cooling	Induction	Brakes	Transmission	Body material	Weight in kg (lb)
3	936	Rear	Flat-6	2142 turbo	83 x 66	ohc	air	injection	discs	Porsche 5+R	polyester	744 (1640)
4	936	Rear	Flat-6	2142 turbo	83 x 66	ohc	air	injection	discs	Porsche 5+R	polyester	757 (1669)
38	935	Rear	Flat-6	2857 turbo	93 x 70.4	ohc	air	injection	discs	Porsche 4+R	steel + polyester	992 (2187)
39	935	Rear	Flat-6	2857 turbo	93 x 70.4	ohc	air	injection	discs	Porsche 4+R	steel + polyester	998 (2200)
40	935	Rear	Flat-6	2857 turbo	93 x 70.4	ohc	air	injection	discs	Porsche 5+R	steel + polyester	986 (2174)
41	935	Rear	Flat-6	2857 turbo	93 x 70.4	ohc	air	injection	discs	Porsche 4+R	steel + polyester	985 (2172)
42	935	Rear	Flat-6	2857 turbo	93 x 70.4	ohc	air	injection	discs	Porsche 4+R	steel + polyester	1009 (2224)
47	Carrera	Rear	Flat-6	2993	95 x 70.4	ohc	air	injection	discs	Porsche 5+R	steel + polyester	979 (2158)
48	Carrera	Rear	Flat-6	2993	95 x 70.4	ohc	air	injection	discs	Porsche 5+R	steel + polyester	978 (2156)
49	Carrera	Rear	Flat-6	3186	98 x 70.4	ohc	air	injection	discs	Porsche 5+R	steel + polyester	918 (2024)
55	934	Rear	Flat-6	2993 turbo	95 x 70.4	ohc	air	injection	discs	Porsche 5+R	steel + polyester	918 (2024)
56	934	Rear	Flat-6	2993 turbo	95 x 70.4	ohc	air	injection	discs	Porsche 5+R	steel + polyester	1132 (2496)
57	934	Rear	Flat-6	2993 turbo	95 x 70.4	ohc	air	injection	discs	Porsche 5+R	steel + polyester	1132 (2500)
58	934	Rear	Flat-6	2993 turbo	95 x 70.4	ohc	air	injection	discs	Porsche 5+R	steel + polyester	1128 (2487)
59	934	Rear	Flat-6	2993 turbo	95 x 70.4	ohc	air	injection	discs	Porsche 5+R	steel + polyester	1132 (2496)
60	934	Rear	Flat-6	2993 turbo	95 x 70.4	ohc	air	injection	discs	Porsche 5+R	steel + polyester	1131 (2493)
61	Carrera	Rear	Flat-6	2993	95 x 70.4	ohc	air	injection	discs	Porsche 5+R	steel + polyester	1003 (2211)
62	Carrera	Rear	Flat-6	2993	95 x 70.4	ohc	air	injection	discs	Porsche 5+R	steel + polyester	957 (2110)
63	Carrera	Rear	Flat-6	2993	95 x 70.4	ohc	air	injection	discs	Porsche 5+R	steel + polyester	963 (2123)
70	Carrera	Rear	Flat-6	2993	95 x 70.4	ohc	air	injection	discs	Porsche 5+R	steel + polyester	990 (2183)
77	Carrera	Rear	Flat-6	2993	95 x 70.4	ohc	air	injection	discs	Porsche 5+R	steel + polyester	992 (2187)
78	Carrera	Rear	Flat-6	2993	95 x 70.4	ohc	air	injection	discs	Porsche 5+R	steel + polyester	980 (2161)
79	Carrera	Rear	Flat-6	2993	95 x 70.4	ohc	air	injection	discs	Porsche 5+R	steel + polyester	1020 (2249)
80	Carrera	Rear	Flat-6	2993	95 x 70.4	ohc	air	injection	discs	Porsche 5+R	steel + polyester	990 (2183)
96	Carrera	Rear	Flat-6	2993	95 x 70.4	ohc	air	injection	discs	Porsche 5+R	steel + polyester	999 (2202)

1978

Twenty-one Porsches start, nine finish and two are unplaced

This was the year that a Renault Alpine won at Le Mans, carrying off the event with brio and panache. The Porsches were never seriously able to trouble the faster and more durable Renaults. However, the Porsche 936/78s had been well prepared in order to meet the French threat. This year the double-turbocharged engines with their four valves per cylinder had air cooling, as usual, for the cylinder blocks, but water cooling for the cylinder heads. None of this, however, was enough to prevent the veteran driver Jean-Pierre Jaussaud and the young prodigy Didier Pironi in their Renault Alpine covering the winning distance of 5044.53km (3134.52 miles) at an average of 210.18km/h (130.60mph).

Porsche no. 6. Type 936/78 (chassis no. 936001), entered by Martini Racing and driven by Barth, Wollek and Ickx. It came second in the distance placings, covering 4968.12km (3087.04 miles) in 24 hours at an average of 207.00km/h (128.62mph).

Always well placed, this 936 had its progress marred by 41 minutes spent in gearbox repairs. After retiring his own car, Jacky Ickx joined this Franco-German team and helped it finish some 80km (50 miles) behind the winners.

Porsche no. 7. Type 936/77 (chassis no. 936002), Group 6, entered by Martini Racing and driven by Haywood, Gregg and Jöst. It came third in distance, covering 4940.73km (3070.02 miles) in 24 hours at an average of 205.86km/h (127.91mph).

A turbocharger change slightly delayed this 'old' 936 (13 minutes), but it maintained its pace to bring it within catching distance of no. 6.

Porsche no. 90. Type 935, IMSA Group, entered by Dick Barbour Racing and driven by Barbour, Redman and Paul. It was placed fifth in distance, covering 4607.42km (2862.91 miles) in 24 hours at an average of 191.97km/h (119.28mph)

This 935 won the IMSA category ahead of all the Group 5 machines. Fitted with a double turbocharger, it led its group from start to finish, by which time it was 59 laps ahead of the runner-up!

Porsche no. 44. Type 935, Group 5, entered by Kremer Racing and driven by Busby, Cord and Knoop. It came sixth in distance, covering 4592.97km (2853.93mph) in 24 hours at an average of 191.37km/h (118/91 mph).

First in Group 5, this 935 with double turbocharger did not suffer any serious mechanical troubles, but its prodigious consumption of oil towards the end of the race caused fears as to whether it would last out.

Porsche no. 41. Type 935, Group 5, entered by A.S.A. Cachia and driven by Guarana, Gomes and Amaral. It was placed seventh in distance, covering 4489.01km (2789.34 miles) in 24 hours at an average of 187.04km/h (116.22mph).

This Porsche, which was in 28th place at the end of the first hour, made few pit stops, never staying for long, with the result that it gradually improved its position throughout the 24 hours.

Porsche no. 43. Type 935/78, Group 5, entered by Martini Racing and driven by Schurti and Stommelen. It finished eighth in the distance classification, covering 4447.73km (2763.69 miles) in 24 hours at an average of 185.32km/h (115.15mph).

Despite its spectacular silhouette 'Moby Dick' was handicapped by its limited range. It was also delayed by all kinds of troubles: the cooling system, the fuel pump, the fuel-injection pump and, finally, exhaust problems.

Porsche no. 66. Type Carrera, Group 4, entered by A.C. Verney and driven by Verney, Lapeyre and Servanin. It came 12th on distance, covering 3817.92km (2372.34 miles) in 24 hours at an average of 159.08km/h (98.84mph).

The winner in Group 4, despite lengthy (15 hours) gearbox repairs. The Carrera, without turbocharger, dominated the 934s in its group that were fitted with turbochargers.

Porsche no. 97. Type Carrera, IMSA Group, entered by Charles Ivey Engineering and driven by Rulon, Miller, Perkins and Spice. It was 14th in the distance classification, covering 3801.15km (2361.92 miles) in 24 hours at an average of 158.36km/h (98.40mph).

Problems with the valve rockers, then with the gearbox, which had to be replaced, held this Porsche back. It came second in its group, but a long way behind the leader.

Porsche no. 62. Type 934, Group 4, entered by 'Segolen' and driven by 'Segolen', Bussi and Briavoine. It was 17th in the distance results, covering 3540.88km (2200.20 miles) in 24 hours at an average of 147.53km/h (91.67mph). The car's

gearbox caused a lot of problems for this team, which came second in Group 4 and was the last to be placed.

Porsche no. 45. Type 935, Group 5, entered by Kremer Racing and driven by Gurdjian, Schornstein and Winter. It was unplaced, having covered an insufficient distance because of engine problems.

Porsche no. 64. Type Carrera, Group 4, entered by Bourdillat and driven by Bourdillat and Bernard. It was unplaced, not having covered the stipulated minimum distance (*ie* 70% of the distance covered by the winner).
The car had driveshaft problems, an oil leak in the gearbox, and various other minor troubles.

Porsche no. 5. Type 936/78, (chassis no. 936003) Group 6, entered by Martini Racing and, driven by Ickx, Pescarolo and Mass. It retired in the 19th hour, after being in 10th place in the preceding hour.

Jochen Mass was driving when the car went out of control opposite Position 121. The rear of the car hit the safety barrier and was too badly damaged to restart. Earlier, precious time had been lost through fuel-injection and ignition problems, as well as changing a fifth gear pinion. Jacky Ickx, as in the previous year, transferred to another car after this retirement — 936, no. 6.

Porsche no. 68. Type 934, Group 4, entered by Hervé Poulain and driven by Holup, Doeren, Poulain and Feitler. It retired in the 16th hour, after being in 31st place in the preceding hour. A jammed gearbox was the cause of this team's retirement: they had already been delayed by changing the turbo.

Porsche no. 69. Type 934, Group 4, entered by Jean-Louis Ravenel and driven by Braillard, Ravenel and Dagoreau. It retired in the eighth hour, after being in 47th place in the preceding hour. Injection pump trouble was the cause.

Porsche no. 65. Type 930, Group 4, entered by Joël Laplacette and driven by Laplacette, Vial, Salamin and Courage. It retired in the 12th hour, after being in 37th place in the preceding hour.

A tyre burst and damaged the brake circuit, which deprived the driver of the ability to slow down at a moment when it was needed. The only 930 entered in the event left the road, and retired.

Porsche no. 48. Type 935, Group 5, entered by Mecarillos Racing and driven by Haldi, Müller and 'Nico'. It retired in the 13th hour, after being in 32nd place in the preceding hour. It had transmission problems.

Porsche no. 91. Type 935, IMSA Group, entered by Dick Barbour Racing and driven by Garretson, Akin and Earle. It retired in the 14th hour, after being in 25th place in the preceding hour.

It was during the night that the second Porsche entered by the Datsun concessionaire, Dick Barbour, left the track and had to be abandoned.

Porsche no. 47. Type 935, Group 5, entered by Gelo Racing and driven by Hezemans and Fitzpatrick. It retired in the third hour, after being in 54th place in the preceding hour.

This 935 had a bad start: it had to stop after one hour to replace a bearing and suspension arm. Finally, at 6.10pm, it went out with sparkplug trouble, starting the list of retirements.

Porsche no. 94. Type 935, IMSA Group, entered by Whittington Brothers and driven by Whittington, Whittington and Konrad. It retired in the eighth hour, after being in 46th place in the preceding hour. This American Porsche was the victim of an accident at 11.15pm on Saturday night.

Porsche no. 61. Type 934, Group 4, entered by Auto Daniel Urcun and driven by Chasseuil, Lefebvre and Mignot. It retired in the sixth hour, after being in 45th place in the preceding hour: a cracked piston was the cause.

Porsche no. 46. Type 935, Group 5, entered by Kremer Racing and driven by Raymond, Franey and Steve. It retired in the third hour after being in 41st place in the preceding hour. This car was in fact nudging 12th place when its engine gave out.

Race no.	Type Model	Engine position	Number of cylinders	Capacity in cc	Bore & stroke in mm	Valve operation	Cooling	Induction	Brakes	Transmission	Body material	Weight in kg (lb)
5	936/78	Rear	Flat-6	2142 turbo	83 x 66	ohc	air + water	injection	discs	Porsche 5+R	polyester	804 (1773)
6	936/78	Rear	Flat-6	2142 turbo	83 x 66	ohc	air + water	injection	discs	Porsche 5+R	polyester	808 (1781)
7	936/77	Rear	Flat-6	2142 turbo	83 x 66	ohc	air + water	injection	discs	Porsche 5+R	polyester	767 (1691)
41	935	Rear	Flat-6	2993 turbo	95 x 70.4	ohc	air + water	injection	discs	Porsche 4+R	steel + polyester	1025 (2260)
43	93578	Rear	Flat-6	3211 turbo	95.7 x 74.4	ohc	air + water	injection	discs	Porsche 4+R	steel + polyester	1054 (2324)
44	935	Rear	Flat-6	2993 turbo	95 x 70.4	ohc	air + water	injection	discs	Porsche 4+R	steel + polyester	1037 (2286)
45	935	Rear	Flat-6	2993 turbo	93 x 70.4	ohc	air + water	injection	discs	Porsche 4+R	steel + polyester	1030 (2271)
46	935	Rear	Flat-6	2993 turbo	95 x 70.4	ohc	air + water	injection	discs	Porsche 4+R	steel + polyester	1032 (2275)
47	935	Rear	Flat-6	2993 turbo	95 x 70.4	ohc	air + water	injection	discs	Porsche 4+R	steel + polyester	1039 (2291)
48	935	Rear	Flat-6	2993 turbo	95 x 70.4	ohc	air + water	injection	discs	Porsche 4+R	steel + polyester	1036 (2284)
61	934	Rear	Flat-6	2993 turbo	95 x 70.4	ohc	air + water	injection	discs	Porsche 4+R	steel + polyester	1127 (2485)
62	934	Rear	Flat-6	2993 turbo	95 x 70.4	ohc	air + water	injection	discs	Porsche 4+R	steel + polyester	1121 (2471)
64	Carrera	Rear	Flat-6	2993	96 x 70.4	ohc	air + water	injection	discs	Porsche 5+R	steel + polyester	980 (2161)
65	930	Rear	Flat-6	3299 turbo	97 x 70.4	ohc	air + water	injection	discs	Porsche 4+R	steel + polyester	1170 (2579)
66	Carrera	Rear	Flat-6	2993	95 x 70.4	ohc	air	injection	discs	Porsche 5+R	steel + polyester	992 (2187)
68	934	Rear	Flat-6	2993 turbo	95 x 70.4	ohc	air	injection	discs	Porsche 4+R	steel + polyester	1156 (2549)
69	934	Rear	Flat-6	2993 turbo	95 x 70.4	ohc	air	injection	discs	Porsche 4+R	steel + polyester	1123 (2476)
90	935	Rear	Flat-6	2993 turbo	95 x 70.4	ohc	air	injection	discs	Porsche 4+R	steel + polyester	1063 (2344)
91	935	Rear	Flat-6	2993 turbo	95 x 70.4	ohc	air	injection	discs	Porsche 4+R	steel + polyester	1104 (2434)
94	935	Rear	Flat-6	2993 turbo	95 x 70.4	ohc	air	injection	discs	Porsche 4+R	steel + polyester	1050 (2315)
97	Carrera	Rear	Flat-6	2993	95 x 70.4	ohc	air	injection	discs	Porsche 5+R	steel + polyester	988 (2178)

1979

Twenty Porsches start, twelve finish

A Porsche was first across the finishing line, but it was not Jacky Ickx's car, as had been expected. Essex, continuing its publicity campaign in the field of motorsport, entered two 936s from the previous year, but they were unable to finish: they had been inadequately prepared. In the end it was a Kremer Porsche 953 K3 that won, a Group 5 car of great sophistication with Kevlar and various other ultra-light materials borrowed from aeronautics employed in its construction.

The event of the year was the distinguished participation of the actor Paul Newman who, thanks above all to his team-mate Stommelen, finished second in the general classification. It should be noted that the conditions were slightly modified in that the course now measured 13.62km (8.46 miles) instead of the 13.64km (8.47 miles) of previous years.

Porsche no. 41. Type 935 K3, Group 5, entered by Porsche Kremer Racing and driven by Ludwig, Whittington and Whittington. It came first in distance, covering 4173.93km precisely (2593.56 miles) in 24 hours at an average of 173.91km/h (108.06mph).

The Kremer men stuck to a very strict regime, and did not seek to duel with the Gelo Porsches. At their own tempo, and from 25 minutes after midnight, the 935 K3 was in first place, and held the lead right to the finish. The only worries were on the Sunday morning when a drivebelt and the fuel-injection pump had to be changed repeatedly. Nevertheless, this car crossed the finishing line seven laps ahead of the second car.

Porsche no. 70. Type 935, IMSA Group, entered by Dick Barbour Racing and driven by Barbour, Newman and Stommelen. It came second in the distance results, covering 4087.81km (2540.05 miles) in 24 hours at an average of 170.32km/h (105.83mph).

Porsche no. 40. Type 935, Group 5, entered by Porsche Kremer Racing and driven by Ferrier, Servanin and Trisconi. It was placed third in distance, covering 3988.25km (2478.18 miles) in 24 hours at an average of 166.16km/h (103.25mph).

An excellent performance from this team, which was not expected to be up to this standard. Third in the general classification and second in Group 5 — a fine effort despite some problems with a defective axle.

Victory in the IMSA Group and second place overall were good reasons for actor Paul Newman to be delighted with his first participation in the Le Mans 24 hours. A slowing up of the leading car galvanised Stommelen, who accelerated and drove hard until slowed by mechanical problems after three hours: unfortunately the front left-hand wheel lost the team 23 minutes and then the turbocharger showed signs of fatigue. Therefore, Stommelen waited until the end of the race was signalled to nurse the car across the finishing line.

Porsche no. 82. Type 934, Group 4, entered by Lubrifilm Racing and driven by Müller, Pallavicini and Vanoli. It came fourth in distance, covering 3972.79km (2468.58 miles) in 24 hours at an average of 165.53km/h (102.85mph).

Herbert Müller and his team-mates were at the front of Group 4 from start to finish, and were 30 laps ahead when the chequered flag went down!

1959 : Porsche 718 RSK.

(Below left) 1971 : Porsche 917. (Below right) 1974 : Porsche 908/2.

1975 : 908/3 (below left). 1976 : 908/3 (below right).

1978 : "Moby Dick".　　　　　　　　　　　1978 : 935 Imsa.

1979 : 936 Essex (above). 1979 : 935 K3 (below).

1980 : 908/80 (left) and 935 K3 (right).

1980 : 924 Carrera GT (above). 1981 : Mass and Ickx cars.

1982 : Porsche Kremer CK5.   1982 : Winning Porsche.

1983 : Porsche 956.

1983 : Porsche Marlboro 956.

1983 : 930 group B.

1984 : Porsche 956.

1984 : Porsche 928.

Porsche no. 42. Type 935, Group 5, entered by Sekurit Racing Team and driven by Schornstein, Dören and von Tschirnhaus. It came seventh in distance, covering 3857.17km (2396.73 miles) in 24 hours at an average of 160.71 km/h (99.86mph).

A very consistent race by the Sekurit Porsche, which progressed through a string of retirements to achieve seventh place overall and third in Group 5.

Porsche no. 72. Type 935, IMSA Group, entered by Dick Barbour Racing and driven by Garretson, Abate and Kitterick. It finished in eighth place on distance, covering 3793.65km (2357.26 miles) in 24 hours at an average of 158.06km/h (98.22mph).

Third in IMSA, this team lost an hour in changing the shock absorbers to all four wheels, then half an hour replacing the damaged spoiler.

Porsche no. 73. Type 935, IMSA Group, entered by Dick Barbour Racing and driven by Kirby, Harmon and Hotchkiss. It came ninth in the distance placings, covering 3748.88km (2329.44 miles) in 24 hours at an average of 156.20km/h (897.06mph). This Kremer 935 had a very steady race some way behind the leaders — nevertheless it secured fourth place in its group.

Porsche no. 43. Type 935, Group 5, entered by Claude Haldi and driven by Haldi, Löwe and Teran. It was 11th in distance, covering 3687.91km (2291.56 miles) in 24 hours at an average of 153.66km/h (95.48mph).

Some 14 minutes before the end of the event Teran drove off the track at Indianapolis corner, damaging the car's bonnet and necessitating some fast work by the mechanics.

Porsche no. 45. Type 935, Group 5, entered by Porsche Kremer Racing and driven by Plankenhorn, Winter and Gurdjian. It came 13th in distance, covering 3655.39km (2271.35 miles) in 24 hours at an average of 152.72km/h (94.89mph). Breakage of a driveshaft pushed this Kremer Porsche back from eighth to thirteenth place just before the end of the race.

Porsche no. 39. Type 935, Group 5, entered by A.S.A. Cachia and driven by Guerin, Alliot and Goujon. It was placed 15th in distance, covering 3610.88km (2247.42 miles) in 24 hours at an average of 150.44km/h (93.48mph).

This 935 was in third place overall when a driveshaft joint failure put paid to its prospects. Earlier, several punctures and a shattered windscreen had not prevented it making a good show.

Porsche no. 86. Type 934, Group 4, entered by Korès Racing and driven by Bourdillat, Ennequin and Bernard. It was 16th in the distance classification, covering 3526.42km (2191.21 miles) in 24 hours at an average of 146.93km/h (93.48mph). It was also second in Group 4, in spite of losing a good hour at the start of the race in changing the water and oil radiators.

Porsche no. 87. Type 934, Group 4, entered by C. Bussi and driven by Bussi and Salam. It retired in the 17th hour, after being in 26th place in the preceding hour. This car was never in contention and withdrew after leaving the track.

Porsche no. 84. Type 934, Group 4, entered by A.C. Verney and driven by Verney, Metge and Bardinon. It was placed 19th in distance, covering 3299.48km (2050.20 miles) in 24 hours at an average of 137.47km/h (85.42mph).

A very long stop handicapped this team. It took 3.5 hours to change the gearbox. Third place in the group was some recompense for these setbacks.

Porsche no. 12. Type 936, (chassis no. 936003), Group 6, entered by Essex Porsche and driven by Ickx and Redman. It was disqualified in the 17th hour, after being in 16th place in the preceding hour.

Ickx set out in front, followed by Wollek and both imposed their pace on the race. After one hour, no. 12 was 2.5 minutes ahead, but at this point trouble with a wheel mounting forced the car to stop for repairs. It was then that Redman overtook, only to burst a tyre: it took him 38 minutes to get back to the pits. The suspension had been affected and 53 minutes were needed for repairs. Ickx and Redman dropped to 35th place but they made a masterly recovery in the rain, reaching 7th position. Unfortunately, the Porsche then stopped again, its alternator drive broken, too far from the pits for any hope of repair.

Porsche no. 14. Type 936 (chassis no. 936001), Group 6, entered by Essex Porsche and driven by Wollek and Haywood. It retired in the 19th hour, after being in 5th place in the preceding hour.

After a brilliant start on the heels of the Ickx-Redman car, this Porsche was held up by induction troubles which compelled the mechanics to change the injection pump. The night was more serene for this team which made up the lost ground, reaching third place before loss of cylinder compression finally put them out.

Porsche no. 36. Type 935, Group 5, entered by Gelo Sportswear and driven by Schurti and Heyer. It retired in the 16th hour, after being in third place in the preceding hour.

The rear left-hand wheel buckled, damaging a suspension link and a stabilizer arm of the Porsche which, at one stage, had been in first place for two hours. In the end the engine overheated and gave out.

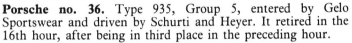

Porsche no. 37. Type 935, entered by Gelo Sportswear and driven by Fitzpatrick, Grohs and Lafosse. It retired in the 16th hour after being in seventh place in the preceding hour. This second Gelo team car withdrew a few minutes after the Schurti-Heyer machine, and for the same reason: engine failure.

Porsche no. 71. Type 935, IMSA Group, entered by Dick Barbour Racing and driven by Akin, McFarlin and Woods. It retired in the fifth hour after being in 24th place in the preceding hour: a faulty cylinder head gasket was the cause.

Porsche no. 68. Type 935, IMSA Group, entered by Interscope Racing and driven by Minter, 'Ted' and Morton. It retired in the 12th hour with engine failure, after being in 18th place in the preceding hour.

Porsche no. 74. Type 935, IMSA Group, entered by Jean-Pierre Jarier and driven by Jarier, Townsend and Touroul. It retired in the third hour, after being in 22nd place in the preceding hour. No luck for Jarier, who was soon out of this race with engine failure.

Race no.	Type Model	Engine position	Number of cylinders	Capacity in cc	Bore & stroke in mm	Valve operation	Cooling	Induction	Brakes	Transmission	Body material	Weight in kg (lb)
12	936	Rear	Flat-6	2140 turbo	87 x 60	ohc	water + air	injection	discs	Porsche 5+R	polyester	820 (1808)
14	936	Rear	Flat-6	2140 turbo	87 x 60	ohc	water + air	injection	discs	Porsche 5+R	polyester	825 (1819)
36	935	Rear	Flat-6	2994 turbo	95 x 70.4	ohc	air	injection	discs	Porsche 4+R	steel + polyester	1083 (2388)
37	935	Rear	Flat-6	2994 turbo	95 x 70.4	ohc	air	injection	discs	Porsche 4+R	steel + polyester	1053 (2321)
39	935	Rear	Flat-6	2994 turbo	95 x 70.4	ohc	air	injection	discs	Porsche 4+R	steel + polyester	1059 (2335)
40	935	Rear	Flat-6	2994 turbo	95 x 70.4	ohc	air	injection	discs	Porsche 4+R	steel + polyester	1037 (2286)
41	935K3	Rear	Flat-6	2994 turbo	95 x 70.4	ohc	air	injection	discs	Porsche 4+R	steel + polyester	1030 (2271)
42	935	Rear	Flat-6	2994 turbo	95 x 70.4	ohc	air	injection	discs	Porsche 4+R	steel + polyester	1036 (2284)
43	935	Rear	Flat-6	2994 turbo	95 x 70.4	ohc	water + air	injection	discs	Porsche 4+R	steel + polyester	1089 (2401)
45	935	Rear	Flat-6	2994 turbo	95 x 70.4	ohc	air	injection	discs	Porsche 4+R	steel + polyester	1029 (2269)
68	935	Rear	Flat-6	2994 turbo	95 x 70.4	ohc	air	injection	discs	Porsche 4+R	steel + polyester	1089 (2401)
70	935	Rear	Flat-6	2994 turbo	95 x 70.4	ohc	air	injection	discs	Porsche 4+R	steel + polyester	1070 (2359)
71	935	Rear	Flat-6	2994 turbo	95 x 70.4	ohc	air	injection	discs	Porsche 4+R	steel + polyester	1049 (2313)
72	935	Rear	Flat-6	2994 turbo	95 x 70.4	ohc	air	injection	discs	Porsche 4+R	steel + polyester	1058 (2332)
73	935	Rear	Flat-6	2994 turbo	95 x 70.4	ohc	air	injection	discs	Porsche 4+R	steel + polyester	1055 (2326)
74	935	Rear	Flat-6	2857 turbo	92.8 x 70.4	ohc	air	injection	discs	Porsche 4+R	steel + polyester	1091 (2405)
82	934	Rear	Flat-6	2994 turbo	95 x 70.4	ohc	air	injection	discs	Porsche 4+R	steel + polyester	1124 (2478)
84	934	Rear	Flat-6	2994 turbo	95 x 70.4	ohc	air	injection	discs	Porsche 4+R	steel + polyester	1106 (2438)
86	934	Rear	Flat-6	2994 turbo	95 x 70.4	ohc	air	injection	discs	Porsche 4+R	steel + polyester	1134 (2501)
87	934	Rear	Flat-6	2994 turbo	95 x 70.4	ohc	air	injection	discs	Porsche 4+R	steel + polyester	1145 (2524)

1980

Twenty-Four Porsches start, ten finish

For the first time in the history of Le Mans 24 Hours, a manufacturer won the event in his own car. Jean Rondeau, the constructor, with team-mate Jean-Pierre Jaussaud, covered 4608.02km (2863.29 miles) at an average of 192km/h (119mph).

The great losers were Jacky Ickx and Porsche. The Zuffenhausen marque was officially absent from Group 6 this year and Ickx had to try for a fifth victory in a 550bhp 936/80 prepared by Jöst. Note the first appearance in the event of a front-engined Porsche (320bhp and four-cylinders in-line), and the brilliantly successful trial with mixed fuel on the single 911SC.

Porsche no. 9. Type 936/80, Group 6, entered by Martini Racing and driven by Ickx and Jöst. It was placed second in the distance classification, covering 4583.30km (2849.93 miles) in 24 hours at an average of 190.97km/h (118.66mph).

After a cautious start in the rain, the 936/80 managed to appropriate first place in both the fourth and in the fifth hours. Unfortunately Ickx had to stop at the Indianapolis corner and change the injection pump drivebelt himself, then restart in sixth place. After a fine recovery he once again put himself in front in the 11th hour, holding the lead until the 19th. Serious gearbox problems then hampered this German-Belgian Porsche and deprived it of victory.

Porsche no. 70. Type 935 K3, IMSA Group, entered by Dick Barbour Racing and driven by Barbour, Fitzpatrick and Redman. It was fifth in the distance placings, covering 4327.05km (2688.71 miles) in 24 hours at an average of 180.29km/h (112.02mph).

Fitzpatrick had been fastest in practice and took command right from the start. The team in the 935 K3 ran an excellent race, slowed by engine trouble at midday on Sunday. Nevertheless they won the IMSA Group.

Porsche no. 73. Type 935 K3, IMSA Group, entered by J.L.P. Racing and driven by Paul, Edwards and Paul. It came ninth in the distance placings, covering 4257.86km (2645.71 miles) in 24 hours at an average of 177.41km/h (110.23mph)

A slight bump two hours before the finish cost 23 minutes in repairing the front suspension. However, the car came second in the IMSA Group after a very consistent race in which it ultimately outstripped the best of the Ferraris.

Porsche no. 4. Type 924 Carrera GT, Group GTP, entered by Porsche System and driven by Barth and Schurti. It came sixth in distance, covering 4310.66km (2678.52 miles) in 24 hours at an average of 179.61km/h (111.60mph).

This was the best of the 924s, driven by a select team. Third in the GTP category, this Porsche damaged its water radiator in the night after an encounter with a rabbit.

Porsche no. 49. Type 935, Group 5, entered by Vegla Racing Team and driven by Schornstein, Grohs and Tschirnhaus. It was in eighth place for distance, covering 4268.35km (2652.23 miles) in 24 hours at an average of 117.84km/h (110.50mph).

This 935 had no serious difficulties in the race and won Group 5. It had proved very fast in practice, rivalling the Porsche no. 70.

Porsche no. 2. Type 924 Carrera GT, Group GTP, entered by Porsche System and driven by Rouse and Dron. It came 12th in distance, covering 4233.73km (2630.72 miles) in 24 hours at an average of 176.40km/h (109.61mph).

All three Porsche 924 Carrera GTs reached the finish. This one was held up only by a very quick sparkplug change — there were only four of them.

Porsche no. 3. Type 924 Carrera GT, Group GTP, entered by Porsche System and driven by Gregg and Holbert. It came 13th in distance, covering 4160.76km (2585.38 miles) in 24 hours at an average of 173.36km/h (107.72mph). This car finished, but did the least well of the three officially entered 924s, being sixth in the GTP class.

Porsche no. 93. Type 911SC, Group 4, entered by T. Perrier and driven by Perrier and Carmillet. It was 16th in the distance placings, covering 3821.60km (2374.63 miles) in 24 hours at an average of 159.23km/h (98.94mph).

This car was interesting for being involved in an offer from ACO to take part in an experiment with mixed fuel (equal parts of alcohol and premium grade petrol). The experiment was a success on all counts, for this old (1977) car made its mark in Group 4 GT. Fuel consumption was apparently 35.6 litres/100 km.

Porsche no. 89. Type 935, IMSA Group, entered by Herve Poulain and driven by Poulain, Snobeck and Destic. It was 20th in the distance placings, covering 3694.97km (2295.95 miles) in 24 hours at an average of 153.97km/h (95.67mph). After a few technical hitches (sparkplugs, change of turbo, repair of wing, etc.), this Porsche finished creditably.

Porsche no. 90. Type 934, Group 4, entered by Bourdillat and driven by Bourdillat, Ennequin and Bernard. It came 24th in distance, covering 3388.85km (2105.73 miles) in 24 hours at an average of 141.20km/h (87.73mph).

This was the last Porsche to be placed. It finished after many difficulties with gearbox and driveshaft joints.

Porsche no. 94. Type 934, Group 4, entered by Almeras Frères and driven by the two Almeras and Höpfner. It retired in the 21st hour, after being in 15th place in the hour before it left the track at the Dunlop bend.

Porsche no. 69. Type 953 K3, IMSA Group, entered by Racing Associates and driven by Akin, Miller and Cooke. It retired with a broken coupling in the 21st hour, after being in 16th place in the preceding hour.

Porsche no. 43. Type 935 K3, Group 5, entered by Porsche Kremer Racing and driven by Verney, Lapeyre and Trintignant. It retired in the 17th hour, after being in 16th place in the preceding hour.

All was going well when Trintignant (the comedian) burst the car's rear left-hand tyre on Hunaudières straight, which sent him into a series of spins. He managed to regain the pits, but the damage was too serious to be repaired.

Porsche no. 91. Type 934, Group 4, entered by A.S.A. Cachia and driven by Bussi, Salam and Grandet. It retired in the 15th hour, after being in 34th place in the preceding hour: a damaged valve was the cause.

Porsche no. 44. Type 935, Group 5, entered by Charles Ivey Racing and driven by Lovett, Wood and Cooper. It retired in the 15th hour with cylinder head gasket problems, after being in 29th place in the preceding hour.

Porsche no. 85. Type 935 K3, IMSA Group, entered by Whittington Bros Racing and driven by Haywood and the Whittington brothers. It retired in the 12th hour, after being in 19th place in the preceding hour. The winners of the previous year had less luck this time: they had to withdraw at 4.14am with a damaged differential.

Porsche no. 45. Type 935, Group 5, entered by Gelo Racing and driven by Wollek and Kelleners. It withdrew in the 15th hour, after being in sixth place in the preceding hour.

In a commanding position during the first three hours, this Porsche was relegated to 17th place after problems with its fuel-injection pump drive. Although a brilliant recovery took it to sixth place, a cylinder head gasket put it out of contest.

Porsche no. 80. Type 934, IMSA Group, entered by Diego Febles Racing and driven by Gonzales, Romero and Febles. It retired in the 14th hour after an accident; it had been in 24th place in the preceding hour.

Porsche no. 42. Type 935 K3, Group 5, entered by Porsche Kremer Racing and driven by Stommelen, Ikusawa and Plankenhorn. It retired in the 13th hour, after being in 20th place in the previous hour. It was the engine that let this team down. Earlier they had already been delayed by fuel-injection pump difficulties.

Porsche no. 71. Type 935 K3, IMSA Group, entered by Dick Barbour Racing and driven by Garretson, Rahal and Moffat. It retired in the 11th hour, with valve problems, after being in eighth place in the preceding hour.

Porsche no. 41. Type 935 K3, Group 5, entered by Team Malardeau-Kremer and driven by Lafosse, Field and Ongais. It retired in the seventh hour with a cracked piston, after being in 20th place in the preceding hour.

Porsche no. 46. Type 935, Group 5, entered by Meccarillos Racing Team and driven by Haldi, Beguin and Merl. It retired with a jammed valve rocker in the fourth hour, after being in 46th place in the preceding hour.

Porsche no. 72. Type 935 K3, IMSA Group, entered by Dick Barbour Racing/Wynn's International and driven by Kirby, Harmon and Scherwin. It retired in the second hour, after being in 52nd place at the end of the first hour.

This was the first Porsche to retire. It hit car no. 20, the Courage-Grand Chevron, which left it in no state to continue the race.

Porsche no. 68. Type 935 K3, IMSA Group, entered by Racing Associates and driven by Mendez, Waiger and Kitterick, It retired in the second hour after an accident at Post 130.

Race no.	Type Model	Engine position	Number of cylinders	Capacity in cc	Bore & stroke in mm	Valve operation	Cooling	Induction	Brakes	Transmission	Body material	Weight in kg (lb)
2	924 Carrera GT	Front	In-line 4	1983 turbo	86.5 x 84.4	ohc	water	injection	discs	Porsche 5+R	steel	944 (2081)
3	924 Carrera GT	Front	In-line 4	1983 turbo	86.5 x 84.4	ohc	water	injection	discs	Porsche 5+R	steel	939 (2070)
4	924 Carrera GT	Front	In-line 4	1983 turbo	86.5 x 84.4	ohc	water	injection	discs	Porsche 5+R	steel	945 (2083)
9	936/80	Rear	Flat-6	2142 turbo	83 x 66	ohc	air	injection	discs	Porsche 6+R	polyester	778 (1715)
41	935K3	Rear	Flat-6	2994 turbo	95 x 70.4	ohc	air	injection	discs	Porsche 4+R	steel + polyester	1032 (2275)
42	935K3	Rear	Flat-6	2994 turbo	95 x 70.4	ohc	air	injection	discs	Porsche 4+R	steel + polyester	1056 (2328)
43	935K3	Rear	Flat-6	2994 turbo	95 x 70.4	ohc	air	injection	discs	Porsche 4+R	steel + polyester	1079 (2379)
44	935K3	Rear	Flat-6	2994 turbo	95 x 70.4	ohc	air	injection	discs	Porsche 4+R	steel + polyester	1053 (2321)
45	935	Rear	Flat-6	3164 turbo	95 x 74.4	ohc	air	injection	discs	Porsche 4+R	steel + polyester	1077 (2374)
46	935	Rear	Flat-6	2857 turbo	92 x 70.4	ohc	air	injection	discs	Porsche 4+R	steel + polyester	1072 (2363)
49	935	Rear	Flat-6	2994 turbo	95 x 70.4	ohc	air	injection	discs	Porsche 4+R	steel + polyester	1050 (2315)
68	935K3	Rear	Flat-6	2994 turbo	95 x 70.4	ohc	air	injection	discs	Porsche 4+R	steel + polyester	1077 (2374)
69	935K3	Rear	Flat-6	2994 turbo	95 x 70.4	ohc	air	injection	discs	Porsche 4+R	steel + polyester	1071 (2374)
70	935K3	Rear	Flat-6	3164 turbo	95 x 74.4	ohc	air	injection	discs	Porsche 4+R	steel + polyester	1031 (2273)
71	935K3	Rear	Flat-6	2994 turbo	95 x 70.4	ohc	air	injection	discs	Porsche 4+R	steel + polyester	1065 (2348)
72	935K3	Rear	Flat-6	2994 turbo	95 x 70.4	ohc	air	injection	discs	Porsche 4+R	steel + polyester	1073 (2366)
73	935K3	Rear	Flat-6	2994 turbo	95 x 70.4	ohc	air	injection	discs	Porsche 4+R	steel + polyester	1086 (2394)
80	934	Rear	Flat-6	2994 turbo	95 x 70.4	ohc	air	injection	discs	Porsche 4+R	steel + polyester	1089 (2401)
85	935K3	Rear	Flat-6	2994 turbo	95 x 70.4	ohc	air	injection	discs	Porsche 4+R	steel + polyester	1076 (2372)
89	935	Rear	Flat-6	2994 turbo	95 x 70.4	ohc	air	injection	discs	Porsche 4+R	steel + polyester	1088 (2399)
90	934	Rear	Flat-6	2994 turbo	95 x 70.4	ohc	air	injection	discs	Porsche 4+R	steel + polyester	1126 (2482)
91	934	Rear	Flat-6	2994 turbo	95 x 70.4	ohc	air	injection	discs	Porsche 4+R	steel + polyester	1126 (2482)
93	911SC	Rear	Flat-6	2994	95 x 70.4	ohc	air	injection	discs	Porsche 5+R	steel	1031 (2273)
94	934	Rear	Flat-6	3299 turbo	97 x 74.4	ohc	air	injection	discs	Porsche 4+R	steel + polyester	1190 (2624)

1981

Eighteen Porsches start, eight finish

A fifth victory for Jacky Ickx at Le Mans — long after he had announced his 'retirement' from motorsport. A victory that was won in the face of high quality opposition. From practice Ickx showed himself to be the best, achieving a lap of 3m 29. 44s, which put him in pole position at the start.

The winning Porsche was basically standard 936, but featured an engine which was a development of the unit designed for the Porsche single-seater intended to race at Indianapolis. Ickx and Bell finished four laps ahead of a Rondeau to win an event saddened by the death of Lafosse and a race steward.

Porsche no. 11. Type 936/81 (chassis no. 936003), Group 6 entered by Porsche System and driven by Ickx and Bell. It won on distance, covering 4825.34km (2998.07 miles) in 24 hours at an average of 201.05km/h (124.92mph).

This car led the race from start to finish without a serious problem, except for a slight difficulty in engaging first gear when starting. Its longest stop did not exceed four minutes. In fact it stopped only for normal maintenance and refuelling.

Porsche no. 55. Type 935, Group 5, entered by Claude Bourgoignie and driven by Cooper, Bourgoignie and Wood. It was fourth in the distance classification, covering 4507.52km (2800.60 miles) in 24 hours at an average of 187.81km/h (116.69mph).

A group victory for this 935 which was hovering around fourth place from the sixth hour. Only a change of bonnet and alternator pulley lost it a few minutes.

Porsche no. 42. Type 935 K3, IMSA Group, entered by Cooke Woods Racing and driven by Verney, Cooke and Garretson. It came sixth in the distance placings, covering 4466.36km (2775.26 miles) in 24 hours at an average of 188.09km/h (116.87mph).

This Porsche contested the lead in its group in the early hours. After a very consistent race, this car was once more in the lead ahead of Andruet's Ferrari when, one hour before the finish, last-minute refuelling cost the Porsche its advantage.

Porsche no. 1. Type 924 GTP, GTP Group, entered by Porsche System and driven by Barth and Röhrl. It was placed seventh in distance, covering 4404.59km (2736.88 miles) in 24 hours at an average of 183.52km/h (114.03mph).

Third in GTP behind the two Rondeaus, this works Porsche ran a very consistent race, making pit stops only for refuelling and normal maintenance.

Porsche no. 60. Type 935/2, Group 5, entered by Vegla Racing Team and driven by Schornstein, Tschirnhaus and Grohs.It came 10th in the distance results, covering 4370.68km (2715.81 miles) in 24 hours at an average of 182.11km/h (113.15mph). The exhaust gave this Porsche serious trouble and delayed it.

Porsche no. 36. Type 924 GTR, IMSA Group, entered by Porsche System and driven by Schurti and Rouse. It was 11th on distance, covering 4302.95km (2673.73 miles) in 24 hours at an average of 179.20km/h (111.35mph). This car finished fourth in its group, despite some gearbox trouble.

Porsche no. 12. Type 936/81 (chassis no. 936001), Group 6, entered by Porsche System and driven by Mass, Schuppan and Haywood. It finished 12th in the distance placings, covering 4253.35km (2642.91 miles) in 24 hours at an average of 177.22km/h (110.12mph).

A faulty sparkplug cost this car 10 minutes at the beginning of the race. It made this up easily (the Rondeaus had problems), but it had to make a long stop (1 hour, 10 minutes) for clutch repairs. Then on the Sunday morning a faulty injection pump delayed it for nearly two hours — which explains its poor position.

Porsche no. 70. Type 934, Group 4, entered by Thierry Perrier and driven by Perrier, Bertapelle and Salam. It was placed 17th in distance, covering 3737.43km (2322.34 miles) in 24 hours at an average of 155.72km/h (96.76mph). This car won Group 4, despite some engine trouble towards the end of the race.

Porsche no. 43. Type 935 K3, Group IMSA, entered by Bob Akin Motor Racing and driven by Akin, Miller and Siebert. It retired in the 24th hour, after being in 10th place in the preceding hour.

There were many checks to this Porsche's progress (exhaust and alternator drive problems) before a short circuit forced its retirement.

Porsche no. 57. Type 935/2, Group 5, entered by Claude Haldi and driven by Haldi, Thatcher and Poulain. It retired in the 22nd hour, after being in 15th place in the preceding hour.

Trouble with the rear axle caused Haldi to spin on the Hunaudiéres straight. The car hit the rails and had to retire.

Porsche no. 40. Type 935, Group IMSA, entered by Jöst Racing and driven by Narvaez, Steckkönig and Miller. It retired in the 13th hour, after being in 18th place in the preceding hour.

It was running very consistently when it caught fire at Post 125, putting an end to its hopes.

Porsche no. 10. Type 917/81, Group 6, entered by Porsche Kremer Racing and driven by Wollek, Lapeyre and Chasseuil. It retired in the eighth hour, after being in 25th place in the preceding hour.

This was one of the great attractions of this year's Le Mans: imagine, a 917 — just like the good old days! Unfortunately Kremer, who built this 'replica' from factory-supplied plans, missed the mark altogether. In performance and roadholding this 917/81 was way behind its glorious forebear. It ended up in the pits with its engine out of commission.

Porsche no. 41. Type 935, Group 5, entered by Preston Henn and driven by Henn, Mignot and Chandler. It retired in the sixth hour, after being in 40th place in the preceding hour. Crankshaft drive breakage forced this K3 out of the race.

Porsche no. 61. Type 935 K3, Group 5, entered by Wera-Meiberg Team and driven by Holup, Dören and Laessig. It retired in the seventh hour, after being in 39th place in the preceding hour.

This car was not in the race for long: running out of fuel put an end to the team's hopes.

Porsche no. 69. Type 935 L1, Group 5, entered by Tuff-Kote and driven by Lundgårdh, Wilds and Plankenhorn. It retired in the sixth hour, after being in 38th place in the hour before its engine failed.

Porsche no. 73. Type 924 GTR, Group 4, entered by Eminence Racing Team and driven by Almeras and Sivel. It retired in the sixth hour, after being booked in 45th place in the preceding hour.

Bad luck struck the Almeras brothers when, two hours after the start of the race, they had to change their car's jammed gearbox. A few hours later came their definitive retirement.

Porsche no. 59. Type 935 K3, Group 5, entered by Porsche Kremer Racing and driven by Field and the two Whittingtons. It retired in the fifth hour, after being in fifth place in the preceding hour.

This car went off like a rocket: but the engine could not take the pressure and blew up.

Porsche no. 14. Type 908/80, Group 6, entered by Jöst Racing and driven by Jöst and Whittington. It withdrew in the fifth hour, after being in 25th place in the preceding hour.

An accident on the Tertre Rouge S-bend put this car out of the race at 7.26pm, when Whittington was at the wheel.

Race no.	Type Model	Engine position	Number of cylinders	Capacity in cc	Bore & stroke in mm	Valve operation	Cooling	Induction	Brakes	Transmission	Body material	Weight in kg (lb)
1	924GTP	Front	In-line 4	2477 turbo	100 x 78.9	ohc	water	injection	discs	Porsche 4+R	steel	998 (2200)
10	917/81	Rear	Flat-12	4909	86 x 70.4	ohc	air	injection	discs	Porsche 4+R	polyester	893 (1969)
11	936/81	Rear	Flat-6	2649 turbo	92 x 66	ohc	water + air	injection	discs	Porsche 4+R	polyester	850 (1874)
12	936/81	Rear	Flat-6	2649 turbo	92 x 66	ohc	water + air	injection	discs	Porsche 4+R	polyester	872 (1922)
14	908/80	Rear	Flat-6	2142 turbo	83 x 66	ohc	air	injection	discs	Porsche 5+R	polyester	787 (1735)
36	924GTR	Front	In-line 4	1984 turbo	86.5 x 84.4	ohc	water	injection	discs	Porsche 5+R	steel	998 (2200)
40	935	Rear	Flat-6	2800 turbo	84 x 66	ohc	air	injection	discs	Porsche 5+R	steel + polyester	1031 (2273)
41	935K3	Rear	Flat-6	2999 turbo	95 x 70.4	ohc	air	injection	discs	Porsche 4+R	steel + polyester	1086 (2394)
42	935K3	Rear	Flat-6	3160 turbo	95 x 74.4	ohc	air	injection	discs	Porsche 4+R	steel + polyester	1098 (2421)
43	935K3	Rear	Flat-6	2999 turbo	95 x 70.4	ohc	air	injection	discs	Porsche 4+R	steel + polyester	1078 (2377)
55	935	Rear	Flat-6	3122 turbo	97 x 70.4	ohc	air	injection	discs	Porsche 4+R	steel + polyester	1060 (2337)
57	935/2	Rear	Flat-6	2992 turbo	95 x 70.4	ohc	air	injection	discs	Porsche 4+R	steel + polyester	1106 (2438)
59	935K3	Rear	Flat-6	3165 turbo	95 x 74.4	ohc	air	injection	discs	Porsche 4+R	steel + polyester	1045 (2304)
60	935/2	Rear	Flat-6	2992 turbo	95 x 70.4	ohc	air	injection	discs	Porsche 4+R	steel + polyester	1071 (2361)
61	935K3	Rear	Flat-6	2992 turbo	95 x 70.4	ohc	air	injection	discs	Porsche 4+R	steel + polyester	1052 (2319)
69	935L1	Rear	Flat-6	1999 turbo	95 x 70.4	ohc	air	injection	discs	Porsche 5+R	steel + polyester	817 (1801)
70	934	Rear	Flat-6	2992 turbo	95 x 70.4	ohc	air	injection	discs	Porsche 4+R	steel + polyester	1137 (2507)
73	924GTR	Front	In-line 4	1984 turbo	86.5 x 84.4	ohc	water	injection	discs	Porsche 5+R	steel	1009 (2224)

1982

Sixteen Porsches start, nine finish

Jacky Ickx won at Le Mans for the sixth time, partnered on this occasion by Derek Bell, for whom this was a third victory. It was a complete triumph for Porsche, with first, second and third places: the three cars crossing the finishing line together, to tumultuous applause.

This year, 1982, will be remembered for it was the first year in which cars competed under the new Group C criteria, involving a limit on fuel consumption. There may have been no premium grade under the new limitation, but there was no shortage of ink! The press, on the whole, not liking this rule, and comparing Jacky Ickx's race to a taxi driver's excursion. However, to be objective, the winning car used the same engine in 1981 (without the fuel limitation) and in 1982 (with the limitation), and this did not prevent the winners beating their previous year's distance record ...

Porsche no. 1. Type 956, Group C, entered by Porsche System and driven by Ickx and Bell. It came first in the distance results covering 4899.68km (3044.52 miles) in 24 hours at an average of 204.12km/h (126.84mph).

Like the two other 956 Rothman Porsches, this car complied with the Group C rules for ground effect. Ickx and Bell executed an uneventful race, holding first place from the ninth hour.

Porsche no. 2. Type 956, Group C, entered by Porsche System and driven by Mass and Schuppan. It came second in distance, covering 4858.16km (3018.72 miles) in 24 hours, at an average of 202.42km/h (125.78mph).

The fiery Jochen Mass would have liked to add a Le Mans victory to his laurels and therefore made a very fast start. However, he had to stop to change a regulator.

Porsche no. 3. Type 956, Group C, entered by Porsche System and driven by Haywood and Holbert. It came third in the distance placings, covering 4640.11km (2883.23 miles) in 24 hours at an average of 193.33km/h (120.13mph).

The third of the Porsche trio. First it lost a door, then a broken rear hub bearing caused further delay. Nevertheless it was there at the finish to enforce Porsche's success ... and take Group C.

Porsche no. 77. Type 935 K3, IMSA/GTX Group, entered by Garretson Development and driven by Verney, Garretson and Ratcliff. It was placed 11th in distance, covering 4074.88km (2532.01 miles) at an average of 169.78km/h (105.50mph).

Porsche no. 78. Type 935 K3, IMSA/GTX Group, entered by BP Cooke Racing and driven by Snobeck, Servanin and Metge. It came fifth in distance, covering 4431.80km (2753.79 miles) in 24 hours at an average of 184.65km/h (114.74mph).

Porsche no. 90. Type 934, Group 4, entered by Richard Cleare Sportscars International and driven by Cleare, Dron and Jones. It was thirteenth in the distance placings, covering 3970.20km (2466.97 miles) in 24 hours at an average of 165.42km/h (102.79mph).

Porsche no. 79. Type 935, IMSA/GTX Group, entered by John Fitzpatrick Racing and driven by Fitzpatrick and Hobbs. It was placed fourth in distance, covering 4488.16km (2788.81 miles) in 24 hours, at an average of 187.00km/h (116.20mph).

A fine performance from this Porsche which reached the finish in a good position, despite the handicap of a defective cylinder from the Sunday morning. It finished first in its group.

Porsche no. 87. Type 924 GTR, IMSA/GTA Group, entered by Goodrich and driven by Bundy and Busby. It came 16th in distance, covering 3714.18km (2307.88 miles) in 24 hours at an average of 154.75km/h (96.16mph).

Porsche no. 60. Type 935 K3, Group 5, entered by Charles Ivey Racing and driven by Cooper, Smith and Bourgoignie. It came eighth in the distance results, covering 4307.31km (2676.43 miles) in 24 hours at an average of 179.47km/h (111.51mph).

Porsche no. 4. Type 936 C, Group C, entered by Belga Team/Jöst Racing and driven by Martin, Martin and Wollek. It retired in the 24th hour, after being in fourth place in the preceding hour.

Porsche no. 75. Type 935, Group 5, entered by Haldi and driven by Haldi, Teran and Hesnault. It withdrew in the 12th hour, after being in 21st place in the preceding hour.

Porsche no. 76. Type 935, IMSA/GTX Group, entered by Bob Akin Motor Racing and driven by Akin, Cowart and Miller. It retired in the second hour, after being in 22nd place in the preceding hour.

An empty fuel tank caused the early withdrawal of this 'Moby Dick' style 935: a connection from the (reserve) fuel pump had broken.

Porsche no. 86. Type 924 GTR, IMSA/GTO Group, driven by Miller, Bedard and Schurti. It retired in the 11th hour, after being in 23rd place in the preceding hour.

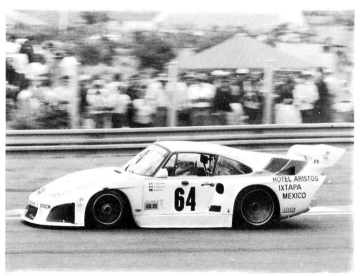

Porsche no. 64. Type 935 K3, Group 5, entered by E. Dören and driven by Dören, Sprowls and Contreras. It retired in the third hour, after being in 21st place in the preceding hour.

Porsche no. 84. Type 924 GTR, IMSA/GTO Group, entered by Canon Cameras/GTI Engineering and driven by Lloyd and Rouse. It was disqualified in the sixth hour, after being in 23rd place in the preceding hour.

Porsche no. 5. Type CK5, Group C, entered by Interscope/Kremer Racing and driven by Field, Ongais and Whittington. It retired in the second hour, after being in 12th place in the preceding hour.

This car was Kremer's response to Group 5: a 936 modified and mounted on a saloon car chassis. A piston that could not stand the pace set by this team forced this interesting car to retire.

Race no.	Type Model	Engine position	Number of cylinders	Capacity in cc	Bore & stroke in mm	Valve operation	Cooling	Induction	Brakes	Transmission	Body material	Weight in kg (lb)
1	956	Rear	Flat-6	2649 turbo	92.3 x 66	ohc	water + air	injection	discs	Porsche 5+R	polyester	858 (1892)
2	956	Rear	Flat-6	2649 turbo	92.3 x 66	ohc	water + air	injection	discs	Porsche 5+R	polyester	866 (1909)
3	956	Rear	Flat-6	2649 turbo	92.3 x 66	ohc	water + air	injection	discs	Porsche 5+R	polyester	868 (1914)
4	936C	Rear	Flat-6	2517 turbo	90 x 66	ohc	air	injection	discs	Porsche 4+R	polyester	878 (1936)
5	CK5	Rear	Flat-6	2394 turbo	92.3 x 70.4	ohc	air	injection	discs	Porsche 5+R	polyester	877 (1933)
60	935K3	Rear	Flat-6	3121 turbo	97 x 70.4	ohc	air	injection	discs	Porsche 4+R	steel + polyester	1042 (2297)
64	935K3	Rear	Flat-6	2844 turbo	92.8 x 70.4	ohc	air	injection	discs	Porsche 4+R	steel + polyester	1046 (2306)
75	935	Rear	Flat-6	2994 turbo	95 x 70.4	ohc	air	injection	discs	Porsche 4+R	steel + polyester	1049 (2313)
76	935	Rear	Flat-6	2994 turbo	95 x 70.4	ohc	air	injection	discs	Porsche 4+R	steel + polyester	1137 (2507)
77	935K3	Rear	Flat-6	2800 turbo	92 x 70.4	ohc	air	injection	discs	Porsche 4+R	steel + polyester	1125 (2480)
78	935K3	Rear	Flat-6	2800 turbo	92 x 70.4	ohc	air	injection	discs	Porsche 4+R	steel + polyester	1096 (2416)
79	935	Rear	Flat-6	2677 turbo	92.8 x 66	ohc	air	injection	discs	Porsche 4+R	steel + polyester	925 (2039)
84	924 GTR	Front	In-line 4	1983 turbo	86.5 x 84.4	ohc	water	injection	discs	Porsche 5+R	steel + polyester	952 (2099)
86	924 GTR	Front	In-line 4	2000 turbo	87 x 84.5	ohc	water	injection	discs	Porsche 5+R	steel + polyester	1077 (2374)
87	924 GTR	Front	In-line 4	2000 turbo	87 x 84.5	ohc	water	injection	discs	Porsche 5+R	steel + polyester	1056 (2328)
90	934	Rear	Flat-6	2993 turbo	95 x 70.4	ohc	air	injection	discs	Porsche 4+R	steel + polyester	1124 (2478)

1983

Twenty-one Porsches start, fifteen finish

On the dawn of the 51st Le Mans 24 Hours it was clear that victory would go to a Porsche again. The big question was to which one? The factory was actually so confident that between practice and the race itself, it withdrew the fourth of the works 956s (no. 33, chassis no. 936004), which would have been driven by Barth and Schuppan. This left three official Porsches. One broke down; the other two finished first and second.

The Rondeaus were never in a position to worry the Porsche fleet, no more than the Lancias, Aston Martins or Saubers: none of these was in the same league. Once again it was a Porsche year.

Porsche no. 3. Type 956 (chassis no. 956004), Group C, entered by Rothmans Porsche and driven by Holbert, Haywood and Schuppan. It came first in the distance placings, covering 5042km (3132.95 miles) in 24 hours at an average of 210.34km/h (130.70mph).

The two Americans (Holbert and Haywood) and the Australian (Schuppan), who were generally unknown to the watching public, won this Le Mans in style. They took the lead in the course of refuelling, but were often very close to being overtaken by Ickx and the suspense at the end of the race grew intense when the Porsche returned to the pits without its left-hand door. The repair was carried out quickly but on the last lap an oil leak put everything in jeopardy: with its oil pressure gone, the Porsche came to a standstill just 20 metres across the finishing line!

116

Porsche no. 1. Type 956 (chassis no. 956005), Group C, entered by Rothmans Porsche and driven by Ickx and Bell. It finished second in the distance placings, covering 5042km (3132.95 miles) in 24 hours at an average of 210.18km/h (130.60mph).

Jacky Ickx was in pole position at the start, after his exploits in practice: a lap of 3m 16.56s, or 249.55km/h (155.06mph). He had not gone far when, on the second lap, he ran into the Lammers Porsche (no. 14) while braking on the Mulsanne: this was where Ickx lost the race. While he returned to the pits for repairs, Mass in car no. 2 broke away, with car no. 3 on his heels. On top of this Porsche no. 1, with Bell at the wheel, came to a standstill on the Mulsanne straight on the Sunday morning: problems in the fusebox. Bell himself made the necessary repair. The two drivers then made a 'qualified' recovery: they made up ground on the leading car but were slowed by their fuel consumption.

Porsche no. 21. Type 956 (chassis no. 956101), Group C, entered by Porsche Kremer Racing, driven by Andretti, Andretti and Alliot. It was placed third in distance, covering 4960km (3082.00 miles) in 24 hours at an average of 206.78km/h (128.48mph).

The Andrettis, always in contention, wanted to pull off a Le Mans win. Unfortunately Mario Andretti was not able to force the pace too much because of the excessive fuel consumption of his car. It was very frustrating for the Formula 1 World Champion not to be able to go after the works Porsche in the lead. Note that this team finished six laps behind the winner and was the first of the privately entered Porsches.

Porsche no. 12. Type 956, Group C, entered by SORGA SA and driven by Schickentanz, Merl and De Narvaez. It came fourth in the distance results, covering 4919km (3056.52 miles) in 24 hours at an average of 205.33km/h (127.58mph).

A splendid car in the 'New Man' colours of yellow, white and black. After tenth-best time in practice it finished with a remarkable fourth place, nine laps behind the winners.

Porsche no. 16. Type 956 (chassis no. 956102) Group C, entered by John Fitzpatrick Racing and driven by Edwards, Keegan and Fitzpatrick. It finished fifth on distance, covering 4878km (3031.04 miles) in 24 hours at an average of 204.63km/h (127.15mph).

In fifth place, 12 laps behind the winners, this Porsche was too thirsty (nearly 50 litres/100km, compared with 44 litres/100km for the more frugal Porsche 956s).

Porsche no. 18. Type 956 (chassis no. 956109) Group C, entered by Obermaier Racing and driven by Lassiga, Plankenhorn and Wilson. It came seventh in the distance placings, covering 4728km (2937.84 miles) in 24 hours at an average of 197.47km/h (122.70mph).

Porsche no. 14. Type 956 (chassis no. 956006) Group C, entered by Canon Racing and driven by Palmer, Lammers and Lloyd. It finished eighth in distance, covering 4619km (2870.11 miles) at an average of 192.57km/h (119.66mph).

Ian Lammers collided with Jacky Ickx braking on the Mulsanne straight. The two cars spun at more than 200km/h (125mph). As a result Lammers lost 2 minutes 50 seconds in the pits repairing the damage. He finished way back, more than 30 laps behind the leaders.

Porsche no. 8. Type 956 (chassis no. 956104) Group C, entered by SORGA SA and driven by Ludwig, Johansson and Wollek. It was sixth in the distance results, covering 4823km (2996.87 miles) at an average of 201.24km/h (125.04mph).

Always in contention, this Porsche had an anxious moment when it ran off the track with some force at the Tertre Rouge S-bend. The front and rear tyres were changed, and damage to the exhausts and radiator had to be repaired. Nevertheless this car finished the event with a creditable placing.

Porsche no. 47. Type 956 (chassis no. 956103) Group C, entered by Fitzpatrick Racing and driven by Henn, Ballot Lena and Schlesser. It came 10th on distance, covering 4456km (2768.83 miles) in 24 hours at an average of 186.04km/h (115.60mph).

This car proved the dark horse of the event and one of the few to accomplish a real recovery: in 47th place at the end of the first hour (after fuel-injection and ignition troubles), it fought back to 10th place behind the eight Porsche 956s and the valiant Sauber.

Porsche no. 93. Type 930, Group B, entered by Charles Ivey racing and driven by Cooper, Smith and Ivey. It was placed 11th in distance, covering 4129km (2565.64 miles) in 24 hours at an average of 172.56km/h (107.23mph).

This car was first in Group B at the end of the first hour, but a BMW M1 took the lead from it. The BMW disappeared; the 930 ran an intelligent race that brought it victory in Group B at the end of the 24 hours.

Porsche no. 92. Type 930 (chassis no. 93A.000171) Group B, entered by Georg Memminger and driven by Memminger, Kuhn, Weiss and Müller. It was placed 13th overall, covering 4074km (2531.46 miles) in 24 hours at an average of 170.03km/h (105.65mph). This car came second in Group B.

Porsche no. 95. Type 930, Group B, entered by Equipe Almeras and driven by Almeras, Almeras and Guillot. It came 15th on distance, covering 3802km (2362.45 miles) in 24 hours at an average of 158.70km/h (98.61mph).

Without doubt this was one of the most aesthetically pleasing cars in this event. The Almeras brothers benefited from their impeccable organization, which took them into third place in their group.

Porsche no. 97. Type 928 S (chassis no. S 840225) Group B, entered by Boutinaud and driven by Gonin, Boutinaud and Le Page. It came 22nd in the distance placings, covering 3188km (1980.93 miles) in 24 hours at an average of 133.01km/h (82.65mph).

No one quite believed it, but yet ... The first Porsche 928 to take part at Le Mans attracted a lot of scepticism at the start. By the finish it had managed to enlist everyone's sympathy. A number of incidents held it up, and a broken hub at the start of the race cost it precious time. Throughout 3000km (1865 miles) this Porsche team wisely let the 956s — faster by 100km/h (62mph) — overtake their car.

Porsche no. 96. Type 930 (chassis no. 930.87.00039) Group B, entered by M. Lateste and driven by Lateste, Bienvault and Touroul. It finished 21st in the distance classification, covering 3597km (2235.07 miles) in 24 hours at an average of 150.56km/h (93.55mph).

Cardan joint trouble all through the race, two punctures on the Hunaudières straight and leaving the road on the new section of the circuit: all of these delayed this Porsche, which crossed the finishing line very battle-scarred.

Porsche no. 94. Type 930 (chassis no. 930.97.00069) Group B, entered by Claude Haldi and driven by Haldi, Stekkönig and Schiller. It was placed 24th in distance, covering 2957km (1837.39 miles) in 24 hours at an average of 137.58km/h (85.49mph). Little success and a series of troubles for the last car in Group B.

Porsche no. 2. Type 956 (chassis no. 956008) Group C, entered by Rothmans Porsche, driven by Mass, Bellof and Barth. It retired in the 22nd hour, after being in 11th place in the preceding hour.

Mass made a very fast start, giving him the quickest lap on his fourth time round. Ickx slowed down and Mass began a sprint which should have carried him to victory. Unfortunately several difficulties held this Porsche back: the ignition first, then trouble with the starter made the team fear the worst with every refuelling stop. It was not until 2.00pm on the Sunday that a cylinder head joint put an end to a very courageous race.

Porsche no. 11. Type 956 (chassis no 956110) Group C, entered by John Fitzpatrick Racing and driven by Fitzpatrick, Hobbs and Quester. It retired in the 10th hour, after being in eighth place in the preceding hour.

Although everything seemed to be going well for this privately-entered Porsche, which had slotted into fourth place behind the factory Porsches, it eventually had to withdraw with fuel pump trouble.

Porsche no. 22. Type CK5, Group C, entered by Porsche Kremer Racing and driven by Jelinski, Warwick and Gaillard. It retired in the seventh hour, after being in 25th place in the preceding hour.

Abandonment, with a ruptured manifold, came at 10.03pm for this Kremer Porsche, which was never among the front runners.

Porsche no. 42. Type CK5 (chassis no. CK501) Group C, entered by Richard Cleare Racing and driven by Cleare, Dron and Jones. It retired in the fifth hour, after being in 42nd place in the preceding hour.

This car's race was over at 4.30pm. After leaving a dense trail of smoke in its wake, it returned at reduced speed to the pits, abandoning the race with turbo trouble at 8.40pm.

Porsche no. 15. Type 956 (chassis no. 936 JR 005) Group C, entered by Jöst Racing Team and driven by Martin, Martin and Duez. It retired in the second hour of the race, after being in 44th place at the end of the first hour. Insoluble fuel-injection problems forced the early retirement (6.00pm) of this Belgian Porsche.

Porsche no. 91. Type 930 (chassis no. 930.8700419) Group B, entered by E. Dören and driven by Yvon, Lemerle and Krankenberg. It retired at 6.46pm, after being in last place at the end of the first two hours.

This 930 was the first of the retirements, after serious gearbox trouble. The box was dismantled, but faced with impossibility of repairing it, this IPAG-sponsored car was pushed out of the pits.

Race no.	Type Model	Engine position	Number of cylinders	Capacity in cc	Bore & stroke in mm	Valve operation	Cooling	Induction	Brakes	Transmission	Body material	Weight in kg (lb)
1	956	Rear	Flat-6	2649 turbo	92.3 x 66	ohc	water + air	injection	discs	Porsche 5+R	polyester	832 (1834)
2	956	Rear	Flat-6	2649 turbo	92.3 x 66	ohc	water + air	injection	discs	Porsche 5+R	polyester	840 (1852)
3	956	Rear	Flat-6	2649 turbo	92.3 x 66	ohc	water + air	injection	discs	Porsche 5+R	polyester	849 (1872)
8	956	Rear	Flat-6	2649 turbo	92.3 x 66	ohc	water + air	injection	discs	Porsche 5+R	polyester	838 (1847)
11	956	Rear	Flat-6	2649 turbo	92.3 x 66	ohc	water + air	injection	discs	Porsche 5+R	polyester	835 (1841)
12	956	Rear	Flat-6	2649 turbo	92.3 x 66	ohc	water + air	injection	discs	Porsche 5+R	polyester	838 (1847)
14	956	Rear	Flat-6	2649 turbo	92.3 x 66	ohc	water + air	injection	discs	Porsche 5+R	polyester	840 (1852)
15	956	Rear	Flat-6	2678 turbo	92.8 x 66	ohc	water + air	injection	discs	Porsche 4+R	polyester	891 (1964)
16	956	Rear	Flat-6	2649 turbo	92.3 x 66	ohc	water + air	injection	discs	Porsche 5+R	polyester	858 (1892)
18	956	Rear	Flat-6	2649 turbo	92.3 x 66	ohc	water + air	injection	discs	Porsche 5+R	polyester	838 (1847)
21	956	Rear	Flat-6	2649 turbo	92.3 x 66	ohc	water + air	injection	discs	Porsche 5+R	polyester	840 (1852)
22	CK5	Rear	Flat-6	2992.5 turbo	95 x 70.4	ohc	air	injection	discs	Porsche 4+R	polyester	827 (1823)
42	CK5	Rear	Flat-6	2992.5 turbo	95 x 70.4	ohc	air	injection	discs	Porsche 4+R	polyester	879 (1938)
47	956	Rear	Flat-6	2649 turbo	92.3 x 66	ohc	water + air	injection	discs	Porsche 5+R	polyester	844 (1861)
91	930	Rear	Flat-6	3185 turbo	98 x 70.4	ohc	air	injection	discs	Porsche 4+R	steel	1235 (2723)
92	930	Rear	Flat-6	3185 turbo	98 x 70.4	ohc	air	injection	discs	Porsche 4+R	steel	1255 (2769)
93	930	Rear	Flat-6	3299 turbo	97 x 74.4	ohc	air	injection	discs	Porsche 4+R	steel	1235 (2723)
94	930	Rear	Flat-6	3299 turbo	97 x 74.4	ohc	air	injection	discs	Porsche 4+R	steel	1258 (2773)
95	930	Rear	Flat-6	3299 turbo	97 x 74.4	ohc	air	injection	discs	Porsche 4+R	steel	1255 (2769)
96	930	Rear	Flat-6	3299 turbo	97 x 74.4	ohc	air	injection	discs	Porsche 5+R	steel	1241 (2736)
97	928S	Front	V8	4664	97 x 78.9	ohc	water	injection	discs	Porsche 5+R	steel	1235 (2723)

1984

Twenty-two Porsches start, twelve finish.

'We are not going to Le Mans, but we are going to win it all the same'. This was the gist of what the Porsche management said to the ACO authorities a few months before the event, when the latter and FISA back-tracked on the rules regarding fuel consumption. Porsche had done a great deal of work in this area which was now wasted, therefore they refused to enter any cars officially at Le Mans.

Porsche-wise, this year's event belonged to the private teams and the ACO. Above all, the race belonged to the spectators, who witnessed an exceptional event during which the leader changed 27 times!

Porsche no. 7. Type 956, Group C, entered by New Man-Jöst Racing and driven by Pescarolo and Ludwig. It took first place in the distance classification, covering 4900.27km (3044.89 miles) in 24 hours at an average of 204.17km/h (126.87mph): it had the fourth best time in practice at 3min 28.42sec.

There were two major incidents for the winning Porsche during the 359 circuits that took it to victory. The first problem came on the second lap when Pescarolo, who had taken the start,

suddenly lost 1500rpm of engine speed through a failure in the fuel-supply system. This was soon put right, but the yellow-and-black Porsche was by then in 30th place; a long way behind the leaders. The other problem for the Jöst team was a damaged suspension component that had to be changed.

The great team of Pescarolo and Ludwig drove a splendidly intelligent and consistent race. Pescarolo deserved this fourth crown to add to his list of honours.

Porsche no. 26. Type 956 (chassis no. 956003), Group C, entered by Henn's T-Bird Swap Shop and driven by Rondeau, Paul Jnr and Henn. It came second in the distance classification, covering 4873.97km (3028.55 miles) in 24 hours at an average of 203.08km/h (126.19mph).

At 7.08am Jean Rondeau, the winning manufacturer of the 1980

Le Mans race, lost his car's front left-hand wheel on the Porsche Bend. Apart from this problem, which could have been much more serious, and having to change a brake disc, nothing of importance occurred to impede the progress of this excellently driven car.

Porsche no. 33. Type 956, Group C, entered by Skoal Bandit Porsche Team, driven by Hobbs, Streiff and Van der Merwe. This car came third in the distance placings, covering 4779.34km (2969.75 miles) in 24 hours at an average of

199.13km/h (123.74mph). A splendid third place for this Skoal Bandit Porsche and a reward for the experience of the veteran Hobbs (who was already driving in 1962, when Philippe Streiff was still a boy).

Porsche no. 9. Type 956, Group C, entered by Brun Motorsport GmbH and driven by Brun, Von Bayern and Akin. It was placed fourth on distance, covering 4628.06km (2875.74 miles) in 24 hours at an average of 192.83km/h (119.82mph).

Porsche no. 12. Type 956T, Group C, entered by Boss Porsche and driven by Merl, Schornstein and 'Winter'. It was placed fifth in the distance classification, covering 4625.72km (2874.29 miles) in 24 hours at an average of 192.73km/h (119.76mph). This Porsche completed 339 laps and was very creditably placed, despite bursting a tyre on the Sunday morning, which necessitated changing a connecting rod.

Porsche no. 11. Type 956, Group C, entered by Porsche Kremer Racing and driven by Jones, Schuppan and Jarier. It came sixth in the distance classification, covering 4591.51km (2853.03 miles) in 24 hours at an average of 191.31km/h (118.87mph).

This Porsche's adventure very nearly turned out badly. After really enlivening the race, engine troubles slowed its progress and the car only re-emerged from the pits in order to complete the last lap.

Porsche no. 20. Type 956, Group C, entered by Team Caggia Porsche and driven by Sigala, Larrauri and Gouhier. It came seventh in the distance classification, covering 4555.61km (2830.72 miles) in 24 hours at an average of 189.81km/h (117.94mph).

A left-hand door, that had to be re-attached at one o'clock in the morning, and trouble with the electronic ignition and the spark plugs, was the fate of this Franco-Italian Porsche.

Porsche no. 17. Type 956, Group C, entered by Porsche Kremer Racing and driven by Needell, Sutherland and French.

It came eighth in distance, covering 4369.39km (2715.01 miles) in 24 hours at an average of 182.05km/h (113.12mph). Needell left the road at 5.43am, after spinning, and touching the rail at the Porsche Bend. Mechanics had to repair the damage before he could restart, but the car ultimately completed 320 laps.

Porsche no. 122. Type 911, Group GTO, entered by Raymond Touroul and driven by Touroul, Bertapelle and Perrier. It was placed 16th in the distance classification, covering 3852.27km (2392.69 miles) in 24 hours at an average of 160.51km/h (99.73mph) – despite the fact that Thierry Perrier broke its rear left-hand wheel. Fortunately he was able to get back to the pits subsequently and rejoin the race.

Porsche no. 123. Type 930, Group GTO, entered by Equipe Almeras Frères and driven by Almeras, Almeras and Winters. It was placed 18th in distance, covering 3669.65km (2275.87 miles) in 24 hours at an average of 152.61km/h (94.82mph).

This car raced in 1983 in Lit National colours. In 1984 it turned in a slightly inferior performance; it was delayed when the turbo had to be taken out.

Porsche no. 106. Type 930 (chassis no. 0879), Group B, entered by Claude Haldi and driven by Haldi, Heger and Krucker. It was placed 19th in distance, covering 3860.16km (2398.59 miles) or 284 laps in 24 hours at an average of 161.67km/h (100.45mph).

Porsche no. 107. Type 928, Group 8, entered by Raymond Boutinaud and driven by Boutinaud, Renault and Guinand. It was placed 20th in the distance classification, covering 3475.99km (2159.88 miles) in 24 hours at an average of 144.83km/h (89.99mph). As in the previous year, this 928 completed the full race.

Porsche no. 34. Type 956, Group C, entered by Team Australia and driven by Perkins and Brock. It retired in the 19th hour, after being in 28th place in the preceding hour. It went out at 1.45am after leaving the road at the Tertre Rouge bend.

Porsche no. 114. Type 930, Group B, entered by Michel Lateste and driven by Lateste, Bienvault and 'Segolen'. It retired in the eighth hour, after being in 42nd place in the preceding hour. A little after 9pm it became apparent that the engine had suffered too much and it seized up. The team had covered 70 laps — 940km (584 miles).

Porsche no. 21. Type 956, Group C, entered by Charles Ivey Racing and driven by De Cadenet, Grice and Craft. It retired in the 22nd hour with engine failure, after being in 13th place in the preceding hour.

Porsche no. 47. Type 956, Group C, entered by Obermaier Racing GmbH and driven by Lassig, Fouche and Graham. It retired in the 18th hour, after being in 27th place in the preceding hour. Delayed by a puncture, then by the changing of a brake disc, this car finally pulled out of the race after an accident at 3.30am.

Porsche no. 61. Type 962, Group C, entered by Henn's T-bird Swap Shop and driven by Ferté, Doren and Henn. It retired in the 22nd hour, after being in 20th place in the preceding hour. Ferté stopped with ignition trouble and retired. With his teammates he had covered 247 laps, or 3366km (2092 miles).

Porsche no. 55. Type 962 (chassis no. 956105), Group C, entered by Skoal Bandit Porsche Team and driven by Keegan, Edwards and Moreno. It retired in the eighth hour after being in 39th place in the preceding hour. It was Keegan who left the road on the 72nd lap, at 9pm, seriously damaging the front suspension and forcing the car's retirement from the race.

Porsche no. 121. Type 930, Group GTO, entered by Charles Ivey Racing and driven by Smith, Smith-Haas and Ovey. It retired in the 19th hour, after being in 29th place in the preceding hour. This car was the winner of Group B in 1983. It had less luck this year for, at the end of 146 laps (1989km/1236 miles), it had to pull out of the race with an oil leak. American, Margie Smith-Haas, was the only woman competing in the 1984 Le Mans.

Porsche no. 16. Type 956 (chassis no. 956007), Group C, entered by GTI Engineering aand driven by Mason, Metge and Lloyd. This car was disqualified at 2.25am, after being in 35th place in the preceding hour. The disqualification was for having restarted with external assistance. Nick Mason, by the way, is Pink Floyd's drummer.

Porsche no. 14. Type 956 (chassis no. 956106), Group C, entered by GTi Engineering and driven by Palmer, Lammers and Lloyd. It retired in the 19th hour, after being in 14th place in the preceding hour. Lammers was at the wheel when the alternator packed up, forcing the car out of the race.

Porsche no. 8. Type 956 (chassis no. 956117), Group C, entered by New Man-Jöst Racing and driven by Schlesser, Johansson and De Narvaez. It retired in the 16th hour after being in 25th place in the preceding hour. Johansson achieved the best practice time of all the Porsches, coming third with 3min 26.10sec behind two Lancia-Martinis.

This 956 made a brilliant start to the race ... until the Swede left

the road on the Hunaudières. He got back to the pits, where the car's bodywork was repaired. From this point onwards the three team-mates moved up towards the lead, but then had to pull out at 4.30am with an overheated engine.

On the Saturday afternoon this car was timed at 347km/h (216mph) on the Hunaudières Straight.

Race no.	Type Model	Engine position	Number of cylinders	Capacity in cc	Bore & stroke in mm	Valve operation	Cooling	Induction	Brakes	Transmission	Body material	Weight in kg (lb)
7	956	Rear	Flat-6	2649 turbo	92.3 x 66	ohc	water + air	injection	discs	Porsche 5+R	polyester	–
8	956	Rear	Flat-6	2649 turbo	92.3 x 66	ohc	water + air	injection	discs	Porsche 5+R	polyester	–
9	956	Rear	Flat-6	2649 turbo	92.3 x 66	ohc	water + air	injection	discs	Porsche 5+R	polyester	–
11	956	Rear	Flat-6	2649 turbo	92.3 x 66	ohc	water + air	injection	discs	Porsche 5+R	polyester	–
12	956	Rear	Flat-6	2649 turbo	92.3 x 66	ohc	water + air	injection	discs	Porsche 5+R	polyester	–
14	956	Rear	Flat-6	2649 turbo	92.3 x 66	ohc	water + air	injection	discs	Porsche 5+R	polyester	–
16	956	Rear	Flat-6	2649 turbo	92.3 x 66	ohc	water + air	injection	discs	Porsche 5+R	polyester	–
17	956	Rear	Flat-6	2649 turbo	92.3 x 66	ohc	water + air	injection	discs	Porsche 5+R	polyester	–
20	956	Rear	Flat-6	2649 turbo	92.3 x 66	ohc	water + air	injection	discs	Porsche 5+R	polyester	860 (1896)
21	956	Rear	Flat-6	2649 turbo	92.3 x 66	ohc	water + air	injection	discs	Porsche 5+R	polyester	860 (1896)
26	956	Rear	Flat-6	2649 turbo	92.3 x 66	ohc	water + air	injection	discs	Porsche 5+R	polyester	850 (1874)
33	956	Rear	Flat-6	2649 turbo	92.3 x 66	ohc	water + air	injection	discs	Porsche 5+R	polyester	–
34	956	Rear	Flat-6	2649 turbo	92.3 x 66	ohc	water + air	injection	discs	Porsche 5+R	polyester	867 (1911)
47	956	Rear	Flat-6	2649 turbo	92.3 x 66	ohc	water + air	injection	discs	Porsche 5+R	polyester	–
55	962	Rear	Flat-6	2649 turbo	92.3 x 66	ohc	water + air	injection	discs	Porsche 5+R	polyester	–
61	962	Rear	Flat-6	2649 turbo	92.3 x 66	ohc	water + air	injection	discs	Porsche 5+R	polyester	–
106	930	Rear	Flat-6	3299 turbo	97 x 74.4	ohc	air	injection	discs	Porsche 4+R	steel	1235 (2723)
107	928	Front	V8	4664	97 x 78.9	ohc	water	injection	discs	Porsche 5+R	steel	1235 (2723)
114	930	Rear	Flat-6	3299 turbo	97 x 74.4	ohc	air	injection	discs	Porsche 4+R	steel	1235 (2723)
121	930	Rear	Flat-6	3299 turbo	97 x 74.4	ohc	air	injection	discs	Porsche 4+R	steel	–
122	911	Rear	Flat-6	3299 turbo	97 x 74.4	ohc	air	injection	discs	Porsche 4+R	steel	–
123	930	Rear	Flat-6	3299 turbo	97 x 74.4	ohc	air	injection	discs	Porsche 4+R	steel	–

Acknowledgements

A number of people have helped me bring this book into being:
● My thanks to the press service of the Automobile Club de l'Quest, and in particular to Monique Bouleux for her patience with me.
● My thanks, too, to all the photographers who have toiled to record all these images on film. I think in particular of Maurice Rosenthal, Philippe Dreux, Jean-Francois Galeron, Thierry Bovy, Pierre Autef, Jean-Michel Dubois, Coppieters, Geoffrey Goddard and many others.
● My thanks to the press service of Porsche (Germany) and in particular to Jürgen Barth.
● Finally, my thanks to Marie-Jeanne Laurent, Anne-Marie Veujoz and Gilles Blanchet who put the original French edition of this book together.

Photo Credits

Achevé d'imprimer sur les presses
de Berger-Levrault à Nancy en septembre 1984
Dépôt légal ; septembre 1984
N° imprimeur 778561-9-84
Imprimé en France